Women in Masjid

Women in Masjid

A Quest for Justice

Ziya Us Salam

Foreword by Dr Syed Zafar Mahmood

BLOOMSBURY

NEW DELHI • LONDON • OXFORD • NEW YORK • SYDNEY

BLOOMSBURY INDIA
Bloomsbury Publishing India Pvt. Ltd
Second Floor, LSC Building No. 4, DDA Complex, Pocket C – 6 & 7,
Vasant Kunj New Delhi 110070

First published in India 2019
This edition published 2026

ISBN: PB: 978-93-6952-662-8; eBook: 978-93-8891-203-7

2 4 6 8 10 9 7 5 3 1

Typeset in Adobe Garamond Manipal Technologies Limited
Printed in India by Manipal Technologies Limited, Manipal

To find out more about our authors and books visit www.bloomsbury.com and sign up for our newsletters

For

Appi (Salma Bi),
whose heart is attached to faith

Contents

Whosoever sees an evil, let him change it with his hand; and if he is not able to do so, then [let him change it] with his tongue; and if he is not able to do so, then with his heart (hold it as hateful in his heart)—and that is the weakest of faith.

—Sahi Muslim

Foreword

The first mosque established by Prophet Muhammad (pbuh) was a multifunctional institution that combined spirituality with education, governance, charity, justice and community building. It was a model of holistic Islamic community living, far broader than the limited function of most modern-day mosques. Keeping half of the population away from such a highly organised socio-religious lifestyle is surely imprudent, yet the reality in most of the world of our times is unsavoury and warrants a closer look.

Against this backdrop, Ziya Us Salam has succinctly brought up the issue of tacit discrimination generally prevalent in the society against women who are supposed to forgo multiple rights, including those of inheritance. As part of his endeavour to restore equal rights to women, he makes a compelling case in this book in their favour by resorting to scriptural and prophetic injunctions. Highlighting the Islamic mandate of 'establishing' (not only offering) prayers (*salah* or namaz), Ziya rightly argues that such a requirement is gender-neutral.

More than fifty times, the Quran asks men and women to 'establish' prayer rather than merely offering prayer. Ziya emphasises that prayer is 'established' in congregation when worshippers stand shoulder to shoulder in submission to the Almighty. He backs this with a quote from Surah Al-e-Imran [verse 43]: 'O Mary, be devoutly obedient to your Lord and prostrate and bow with those who bow (in prayer).'

Praying in *jamaat* (collective) five times a day is mandatory for men and optional for women. Ziya says it is like a brick supporting another brick to raise a wall and ultimately completing a building; a solitary brick by itself has limited use. Congregational prayers are as significant for women as they are for men. And that can happen best through the institution of masjid. That ensures the benefits of sorority even as it promotes the robust spiritual existence of women. Denying these is tantamount to 'innovation in matters of faith' and that is misguidance.

However, the book clarifies that for women (unlike for men) praying in congregation is a right, not a duty, as stated by the noted Islamic scholar of the 20th century Mufti Abdul Dayam in *Tajreed Bukhari Sharif*. Dayam quoted Umm Salama, 'When the Prophet would conclude prayer with "salaam" then women would get up and leave. And the Prophet would wait for a little time before getting up.'

Free and equal participation of women in the massive congregational prayers regularly held in the grand mosques at Makkah and Medina, Islam's holiest shrines, should suffice to send the right egalitarian message across the globe. In fact one of the doors in Al-Masjid al-Nabawi is named 'Baab-al-Nisa' (Door of Women). This spiritual and logistic strand has metamorphosed and widely seeped into the Arab culture in general and in the Muslim societies of Southeast Asia, and more so on both sides of the Atlantic. In Turkey most mosques keep abayas (cloaks for women to cover themselves). However, as Ziya rightly laments, the anti-women syndrome is specific to the Indian subcontinent, with sporadic exceptions mostly among the Ahle Hadis. In some families of the subcontinent women do solemnly cover their heads with a dupatta as a mark of respect when the nearby muezzin calls the azan.

Within the mosques where women participate in the prayers there is much to mull over their topological placement in the sacred precincts. While both men and women are under spiritual injunction to wear the most decent clothes in the mosque, the women surely deserve additional care and protection. One way is that they stand behind the men so that during the prayers men concentrate with single-minded devotion to the divine calling. Yet Ziya notes that some schools of Islamic jurisprudence such as the Maliki school—most common in the West—discourage women being imams. Other schools accept women imams, but they are allowed to lead prayers only in front of women.

The author's bracketing of women's right to pray in the mosque with the Prophet's tradition declaring husband and wife as mutual partners and that the mother deserves three times additional reverence than the father provides to the believers potential food for thought. So does his highlighting of the azan as a call to believers irrespective of their gender.

Ziya reminds readers that a vital part of pilgrimage is Sa'ee, walking between two hillocks seven times, which recalls a woman's motherly perseverance. He touches upon the larger cosmic purpose of the congregational prayers—five times daily in the neighbourhood mosque, once a week (on Fridays) in a bigger mosque, Eid prayers in a much larger setting and the once-in-lifetime prayers at the global gathering in Hijaz. And he appealingly intertwines this with the rational necessity to unite humanity inter se, without prejudice towards either gender. He sees the Hajj as an annual mass message for gender justice.

Ziya holds in high esteem the practice currently prevalent in the US where almost every mosque is inclusive, where both men and women are welcome. He quotes a statement by the Islamic Society of North America that reads: 'Hadith confirms that in the Prophet's masjid women prayed salah regularly, attended Jum'ah prayer, made optional prayer (nawafil), did itikaf in the masjid during Ramadan, and met in the masjid.' He also found out that in China women led the prayers some 600 years ago.

In any case, to help facilitate a healthy environment and avoid fitna (temptation), the Messenger of Allah instructed both men and women not only to dress adequately but also to lower their gaze and guard their modesty. When the Prophet led prayers, men stood in a row behind him and the women stood behind men in their own row. Each row was exclusive to one gender. The mixed-gender rows could well be the innovation the Prophet warned about.

Nonetheless, Ziya advocates improvement in this regard in many mosques in the UK. In 2018, the lead was taken by some Scottish women who went from mosque to mosque pleading for equal prayer space and a place on the decision-making bodies. As a result, the Muslim Council of Britain came up with a programme for training women to run mosques. In France women are seeking entry to the main prayer halls. Europe's first all-women's mosque in Denmark is named after Christ's mother, Mariam, the only lady to have a Quranic chapter named after her. The South African organisation Women of Waqf has managed to get better praying space in some mosques or the permission to stand behind men in a gallery in other mosques.

I share Ziya's concern that the original multifaceted purposes of masjids are not being fulfilled by Muslims. The Prophet used the mosque for spiritual as well as worldly betterment of the society. It was the centre of community life, a place of spirituality, learning, governance and social welfare. In addition to the Quran and sunnah, he educated the people in ethics and law, responded to queries on all matters of life, gave regular sermons, including the Friday khutbah, and narrated stories of previous prophets and others to impart moral lessons. He held consultations with companions on community affairs, resolved disputes, hosted delegations and negotiated treaties. He got charity, food and other resources disbursed from the mosque, and provided shelter to the homeless. He acted as a mediator between tribes in conflict. Sadaqah and zakat were often collected and distributed from the mosque. Refugees were supported and resettled through mosque-based networks.

This continued later too. Cairo's Al-Azhar Mosque, established in 10th century AD, is the oldest continuously operating university in the world. It provided free food, lodging and education for thousands of students from all over the world. Interfaith discussions were made there. Earlier, Qarawiyyin Mosque in Fez (Morocco), established in the mid-9th century AD, too provided free education in science, medicine and religion. Here, non-Muslims and women had access to libraries and lectures, the library at one time home to one of the richest manuscript collections in the world. Incidentally, it was a woman, Fatima al-Fihriyah, who funded and founded this entire mosque-university complex for public welfare.

The Umayyad Mosque in Damascus was the central hub for religious and scientific studies. Many mosques in Damascus were networked with bīmāristāns (hospitals). The Süleymaniye Mosque in Istanbul organised a massive Waqf system. It financed soup kitchens, hospitals, schools, caravanserai and bathhouses. These were also linked to healthcare for the poor and hygiene promotion. The Jama Masjid in Delhi often served as a shelter during disasters like famines during the Mughal era. Mosques in the UK and the US continue such social work and provide food banks and homeless shelters. Many mosques organise vaccination drives, blood donation and health screenings, refugee assistance and counselling, interfaith programmes and climate care activism.

Ziya thus deserves accolades for highlighting the ummah's collective dereliction in keeping half of its members away from masjids. Reconnecting women with mosques would surely help to go back to the roots and rejuvenate the basic Islamic ethos. It has to be an internally well-supported community exercise ... that's what the author has contributed to. Ziya joins the ranks of others who have written on similar subjects, such as Marion Holmes Katz, Tazeen M. Ali, Jasser Auda, A.K. Nadwi and N. Reda. The current book, with purity of thought, takes the discussion forward in the context of the Indian subcontinent.

Dr Syed Zafar Mahmood
President, Zakat Foundation of India

Preface

It is a cold, bleak winter evening in Nainital. The tourists are on their way back to their hotels for a night of warmth and pleasure. A few young men among them, however, take time out to offer Isha prayers at a mosque near Mall Road. The mosque offers warm water for ablution and a fully carpeted praying area, making it that little bit easier for devotees. Women, though, are not as fortunate. Even as their husbands offer their prayers indoors, the wives stand and wait for them outside. There is no provision for women to offer prayers inside the mosque. Those who wish to pray, they have no alternative but to do so in the seclusion of their hotel rooms. The mosque accommodates no women.

Nainital is no rarity. It is the same everywhere, from the mountains and hills to the plains, the deserts or the coasts. Men monopolise the mosques and women hardly make an attempt to reclaim what is rightfully theirs. Call it indoctrination or sheer ignorance. But this is the reality of India: more than 95 per cent of the mosques are a no-go zone for women.

Sample this: It is 2007 and the Pakistan cricket team is in India. Some players from the Indian and Pakistan teams wish to offer Friday prayers at the Jama Masjid in Kolkata. The administration makes due arrangements. The players offer their prayers, sign a few autographs and come back to the safety of their team bus. Their wives stay back in the hotel. They do so as much because of lack of provision for women to offer prayers in the mosque, as the lack of awareness about their rights. Incidentally, the picture is not too different in Bangladesh, where many hotels offer facilities to men to offer prayers together. A room or hall is usually reserved for the purpose. Yet, no such facility is extended to women; the underlying belief being they would pray in their room, if at all.

Or take this: Anwar Ali Khan, a middle-class man from Nizamuddin in New Delhi, is out shopping with his wife and children at New Delhi's Connaught Place. As the family moves from one shop to another, the muezzin's call for prayer from the Salam Masjid nearby pierces the air. It is time for Asar, or the early evening prayer. Khan immediately leaves his shopping bags in the custody of his wife and ten-year-old daughter to head to the Salam Masjid. As he offers his prayer, his wife and daughter bide their time, doing some window shopping. They also would like to offer their prayers, but the mosque accommodates only men. A rare woman who might insist on offering her prayer is just about tolerated, but given clearly unwelcoming looks, and ends up hurriedly completing her salat. As she leaves the mosque, it is not unusual to hear many a man call it the sign of impending Doom's Day!

Now, let's take a look into the life of Shaziya, a scholar of political science. Clearly Leftist by political leanings, she insists that her husband take their ten-year-old son to the Aligarh Muslim University's mosque when he goes out for the Friday prayers. It does not strike her that her twelve-year-old daughter deserves a similar exposure.

Or take the case of Ikhlasi Begum. Married to a renowned Islamic scholar, and having spent a good many years living in a house adjacent to a mosque in Old Delhi, it took her all the years till the age of seventy-six, and an excursion all the way to New Delhi's Jama Masjid, to offer her maiden Eid prayers!

This reality of everyday life in India is in stark contrast to what the Prophet stood for. It would be worthwhile to remember that around the time Prophet Muhammad was born in 570 AD, the girl child enjoyed no right to life in the Arab world. Many were buried alive. The lucky ones who escaped death at the time of their birth had no right to property or to seek education, etc. It changed with the coming of the Prophet. After the first revelation to Prophet Muhammad in 610, the situation for women began to get better. By 632, the year the Prophet bade goodbye to the world, women's condition, at least in the Arab world, had substantially improved. They not only regained the right to life, putting an end to the abominable practice of female infanticide, the Quran conferred upon them the right to seek education, the right to own and manage their property, etc. They had a right to their parents' property as also that of their husband. Besides enjoying a right over their earning—the husband had zero control or say in the matter—women also had the right over their husband's income. And if the husband was not earning enough, the wife could give him zakat (poor due) too! Of course, she continued to be the sole owner and disposer of her wealth. As a young girl, she sought education. As an adult, her permission was essential for a nikah to be solemnised. As a married woman, she retained her maiden name. Women began to be masters of their destiny. Indeed, Khadijah, the first wife of the Prophet, was at one time his employer too, her riches outweighing those of the men in the Arab world. The first person to believe in the Prophet was not a man, but a woman, his wife Khadijah. Many years later, the Prophet's youngest wife, Ayesha, used to be his constant companion as caravans set out in the desert. Women also came to mosques, at dawn or dusk. No exceptions were made. They listened to sermons at the Prophet's mosque; they gave sermons too, where both men and women listened to them.

Contrast that with the many centuries it took for Europe or the US to confer elementary rights on women. It was only in 1835 that in the American states of Massachusetts and Tennessee a married woman was given the right to own or manage her own property. This too was dependent on the incapacity of her husband. The other states took even longer to grant this limited right. It was the same with a woman's earnings. Not until 1861 were women granted independent rights over their income. It is pertinent to recall that all along there was a vast disparity in the earnings of men and women. For the same work, women were paid much less than men. Shockingly, it was as recently as 2005 that the former world's number one women tennis player Venus Williams gave a rousing speech at Wimbledon, beseeching men among the organisers to pay women the same as they did men! This is when women had been playing at Wimbledon since 1880! Williams said,

> Close your eyes. Imagine you are a little girl. You're growing up. You practise as hard as you can, with girls, with boys. You have a dream. You work as hard as anyone you know. And then you get to this stage, and you're told you're not the same as a boy. Almost as good. But not quite the same. Think how devastating and demoralising that could be.

That year, as the winner of the women's crown, she took home $1.08 million. The men's section winner Roger Federer won $1.13 million. Her heartfelt words granted Williams a place in the annals of gender parity, but in 2005 many men protested. Besides the organisers, some openly contended that women did not work as hard and did not deserve the same pay cheque. Williams put her career at stake by sticking her neck out. In 2007, her efforts bore fruit. Both men and women players were paid equally at the tradition-bound Wimbledon.

If this was the situation at a tennis tournament, albeit a premier one, in 2005, imagine the uproar the Prophet's teachings and the message of the Quran would have created in the 7th century when to be illiterate was to be normal. Men, who called the shots in Makkah and Medina, were hugely upset when the Prophet talked of property rights for women or giving women an equal right to education. The Prophet was called names. The worst form of slander was resorted to. Violence was not abjured either. Patriarchy was well and truly challenged. The Prophet and his companions set about giving us a new social order, where women were not discriminated against and men were held accountable.

That was then. Cut to the Indian Muslim society in 2025. Women, as half of the ummah, experience what can only be described as a saga of tacit discrimination. In every sphere of life, it is women who are supposed to forgo their rights. For instance, in their parental house, girls are often actively encouraged to give up their claims to inheritance. The argument usually being, 'What will you do with this property? You are likely to go away after marriage.' Same at the time of nikah, where women are often encouraged to surrender their mahr—loosely, dower or woman's due; the term adopted being a patronising 'maaf kar dena' (to pardon). This is expected not for a husband who does not have the means to give her due, but for a husband who may otherwise be well off. Yet, it is the woman who is asked to forgo her right. Men as brothers are never asked to surrender their rights to ancestral property; as husbands they are not encouraged to give their wives more than their mahr due. The silent deprivation does not end with marriage. It continues even after the husband dies. As widows, women are usually asked to give their share to the children. After all, they have a future ahead of them! This tendency to deprive women under whatever pretext manifests periodically, from pursuing higher education to travelling alone. Or even going to the local mosque for prayer. Again and again, women are reminded of only one Hadith, wherein the Prophet is reported to have said that the best prayer for a woman is in the inner room of her house. The text is readily aired, but the context almost never applied!

It is the same when women in the Indian subcontinent are reminded about the alleged preference of Caliph Umar for women to pray at home. Half knowledge can be dangerous. The Caliph made no such prohibition, nor did the Quran. And the Prophet never forbade women from going to mosques. Yet under the garb of religion, patriarchal forces continue to deprive women of their right to enter the mosques, pray alongside their sisters and reap the benefits of sorority, just as men bond with each other. The religion that sought to put an end to discrimination and exploitation of women is now selectively used to perpetuate deprivation and dispossession of women. That this, like in the case of instant triple talaq, goes against the very teachings of the Quran and the Prophet seems to have been forgotten.

Incidentally, while women are often, and erroneously, reminded that their best prayer is performed at home, selective amnesia overtakes society when it comes to talking of the condition of women during the time of the Prophet. Or even the days of Caliph Umar. During his time, women not only went to the mosques, but also participated in battles! Women are never told that the same caliph appointed a well-known female companion al-Shifa bint Abdullah Al-Adawiyyah as the Supervisor of the Markets of Medina. She was appointed not because of the dearth of able men, but because she was more meritorious, with better leadership skills. She used to go to the Medina markets with a whip in her hand, ready to strike at any indiscretion. No companion of the Prophet objected to her lofty status.

As for Caliph Umar himself, well, he was the imam of the Prophet's Mosque. But he did not stop his wife from praying in the mosque. According to Sahi Bukhari Hadith,

> The wife of Umar used to go to the mosque (Al-Masjid al-Nabawi) for the prayers of Fajr and Isha. It was said to her, 'Why do you go out when you know that Umar doesn't like it.' She said, 'What stops him from forbidding me?' It was said to her, 'What stops him, is the saying of the Prophet who said, "Do not stop the women from the Masajid (mosques) of Allah".'

No, the caliph did not forbid women from going to the mosques and praying there, or even giving a sermon. He followed the Prophet's instruction. It is the men in the 21st century Indian subcontinent who do that. Not the Prophet. Not the caliphs. Not the Quran, but ill-informed men drunk on potions of male superiority, a society where men decide and women follow, where men instruct and women obey. Sociocultural mores rather than religious dictates are at play, as is the incomplete and lopsided knowledge of the scriptures. To this, noted Islamic scholar Dr Israr Ahmad said, 'The backward and ignorant Muslims have imposed their own self-forged model upon the Muslim woman. This model has indeed reduced the Muslim woman to merely a beast of household burdens and a sex-maid, and imperceptibly negates and denies her independent spiritual existence.'[1]

The immutable instruction of the Almighty was completed with the revelation of the Quran. In verse 3 of Surah Maida, it is said, 'This day, I have perfected your religion for you, completed My Favour upon you, and have chosen for you Islam as your religion.' After the revelation of this verse, no argument can hold about 'the Prophet's times were different' or that 'men were more decent and pious', etc. The fundamental principles of the Quran remain valid for all times to come. Suggesting that one can pick and choose verses to follow according to preference is tantamount to rebellion. Prophet Ibrahim did not pick and choose the Lord's instructions to follow, nor did Prophet Lot. Or Prophet Nooh. The Quran has to be followed in letter and spirit. Moving away from the message of the Quran amounts to going astray. As the Prophet himself said, 'Every innovation (in matters of faith) is misguidance, and every (one practising) misguidance will be in the Fire.' Barring women from the mosques is an innovation one can do without.

It is time for women to reclaim the space they have surrendered. And time for men to stand up against this injustice perpetuated in the name of faith. It is especially relevant today for people of all genders to have access to places of worship and avenues of self-realisation. Opening the doors of the mosques goes beyond the cry of gender justice and it reaches the realms of human justice. The faithful believe Allah is Adil, one who does justice. Excluding 50

---

[1] Ahmad, Israr. 2003. *Religious Obligations of Muslim Women*. Lahore: Markazi Anjuman Khuddam ul Quran.

per cent of the society from the avenues of self-realisation leads to debilitation of the community, besides being an obvious injustice towards women. If the community fails to take quick remedial measures, it could well be staring at another triple talaq-kind of situation, where right wing hawks will masquerade as well-wishers of Muslim women, pushing the Muslim men into an indefensible situation. Men can then draw sustenance neither from the Quran, as in the case of the Shayara Bano versus the Union of India judgement, popular as the triple talaq judgement in the mind of the common Indian, nor from the larger Indian society. Or even from the mosques all over the world.

This deliberate exclusion of women from the mosques does not happen in the Arab world. Women enjoy complete right to go to Al-Masjid al-Nabawi, Al-Haram or any other mosque in Saudi Arabia, the United Arab Emirates (UAE), Qatar, etc. It is the same with women in the Muslim countries of South-East Asia, for example, Indonesia or Malaysia. Women in most European countries and the US do not face this embargo, where mosques are often used as sociocultural centres for both men and women. This discrimination seems to be reserved only for women in India, Pakistan and Bangladesh. In the Indian subcontinent, most mosques are out of bounds for women, except some in Kerala or others maintained by the minority Ahl-e-Hadith sect. Pertinently, women enjoyed much greater freedom during the days of the Delhi Sultanate and the Mughals. Many royal women were known to have built imperial mosques; many mosques, from Delhi to Bengal, had sections reserved for women to come and pray. It all changed with the decline of the Mughals and the coming of the British. As conservative, orthodox elements raised the cry of religion being in danger, women were the first to be sent into the closet. They have not emerged from there ever since.

Women in Masjid: A Quest for Justice is a small attempt at righting a historical wrong. Here an attempt has been made to project the reality of women's rights and responsibilities in Islam, drawing from the reservoir of history and religion. Also, the book projects the comparative reality of women's access to the mosques across the world, the enlightened ones in West Asia and the West, to the more traditional ones from the subcontinent. Some brave women, having ducked the odds to carve out their own space in matters of faith, help in taking the narrative forward. Yet for any change to be ushered in, it is essential to realise that something is wrong in the first place. The Indian Muslim society, with honourable exceptions, is yet to come to the point where it realises the wrongs perpetuated on 50 per cent of the society in the name of Islam. Most women themselves remain either ignorant or indoctrinated. It is in light of this hurdle that a handful of men and women seeking to restore parity need to be given a helping hand. As the Prophet said, 'Here is an endeavour to move from the weakest to a slightly higher level of faith.'

Acknowledgements

This book would not have been a reality without the steadfast support of my wife Uzma who shared with me her inputs and experiences as a woman. Or my daughters Maryam and Aliza who seek every opportunity to go to the mosque on Fridays. I got ready and impeccable support from my brother Tausief Ausaf who used a fine comb to go through the chapters related to West Asia. He also enlightened me with the realities of the mosques in Jeddah. I would like to thank my friend of many years Anjana Rajan who exhibited all her patience and skills in reading some of the chapters. I have to nod in gratitude to my sisters Salma, Muslima and Sajida, all of them shared with me stories of their lived Islam, some pleasing and others disconcerting. Same for my brother Tauqueer, based in Riyadh, he never failed to urge me on and always asked about the progress of the project. Also, my old pillar of strength Aftab Alam helped by taking special pictures on a trip to Indonesia. My nieces and nephews Ruby, Osama, Samia, Yasir, Umair, Humera Hayat and brothers Shahid Ali, Danish Salim and Junaid Ali Syed all chipped in with their inputs, and, at times, through photographs of the mosques in their respective cities. Not to forget the good wishes of my friends Mohammed Zubair, Irfan Ahmad, Mansoor Ansari, Mushtaq Ahmad, Aslam Khan, Masroor Mian and Brother Zubair Iqbal Khan who took me around Riyadh mosques. I also relied on the treasure trove of *ilm* of Islam of Dr M. Aslam Parvaiz. Grateful, I have to thank the helping hand extended by my old friend Soumik

Mukhopadhyay who made available some rare photographs of hajj, and the well-known Islamic scholar Muhsin Hendricks who shared more than just a photograph from South Africa. Nor can I afford to forget my friends and colleagues at *The Hindu* and *Frontline*, particularly Shailaja Tripathi, Anuj Kumar, Venkitesh Ramakrishnan, V. Venkatesan, Divya Trivedi and Purnima Tripathi. I cannot forget the support of everybody at Bloomsbury, right from Praveen Tiwari Sahab who discussed the proposal with me with the frankness of an old friend, and Kunal Jalali Sahab who introduced me to him, to my editors Shreya Chakraborti and Jaishree Ram Mohan. With their clear mindset and an ability to find quick solutions, they added to the narrative of the book.

Finally, this project, like my prayers, would not have been completed without the support of my brother Khadim Hussain. He seldom meets me, but helps me constantly, and is really the best of persons.

The believing men and women are protectors and helpers of each other. They (collaborate) to promote all that is good and oppose all that is evil; establish prayers and give charity, and obey Allah and his Messenger. Those are the people whom Allah would grant mercy. Indeed, Allah is Exalted and Wise.

—Al-Taubah [verse 9:71]

CHAPTER 1

Through the Lens of Faith

Islam does not discriminate between men and women. Why do men?

The Quran regards men and women to be each other's partners. It clearly tells the husbands that their wives have the same rights unto them as they have unto them. Except that men are a degree superior. This one-degree superiority of men, meant to resolve any deadlock in a marital relationship, has been turned into a 360-degree advantage by men across the Indian subcontinent. The Quran asks men and women to establish prayer, through Surah Tawbah [verse 71], besides around sixty other places. It asks both men and women to pay zakat, that is, poor due. It makes no distinction on the basis that women may not be professionals, or earning a salary at the end of the month. The Quran expects both men and women to perform hajj once in a lifetime, their resources and health permitting. At no place does the Quran put impediments in the path of women. No matrimonial match can be solemnised without the woman's consent. If it comes to divorce, the Quran provides the woman a way out too. After divorce, men are told that a woman is free to do what she chooses to do with herself. Neither first marriage nor second marriage nor remarriage can be conducted without the woman's independent will.

Pertinently, the Quran treats pious men and women equally. In fact, through Surah Ahzab it tells us that there are rewards for both believing men and believing women, chaste men and chaste women, etc. Likewise, for men given to promiscuity, there are similar women. In this respect, particularly telling are three verses, 34 to 36, of the Surah that put things in perspective and give ten traits of equality between men and women. Though technically, these verses are addressed to the wives of the Prophet, they are applicable to all Muslim women. Here, verse 34 of Surah Ahzab clearly states, 'And bear in mind that which is recited in your houses of the revelations of Allah and wisdom. Lo, Allah is Subtle, Aware.' The next verse talks clearly about believing men and believing women, making no distinction on the basis of gender and promises equal rewards to both for their good actions. It states,

> Indeed, the Muslim men and Muslim women, the believing men and believing women, the obedient men and obedient women, the truthful men and truthful women, the patient men and patient women, the humble men and the humble women, the charitable men and the charitable women, the fasting men and fasting women, the men who guard their private parts and the women who do so, and the men who remember Allah often and the women who do so—for them Allah has prepared forgiveness and a great reward.

So, there is equal reward for a truthful person, irrespective of the gender. Same goes for acts of charity, fasting, modesty, etc. Will God discriminate on the basis of gender when it comes to salat, the daily prayer, or special prayers like Friday, or Taraweeh? No. He does not. The Quran through Surah Dhariyat says, 'I created the jinn and humankind only that they might worship Me.' The Prophet actively encouraged women to offer Friday prayers and those on Eid in a congregation.

In Islam, whether a man or a woman goes on hajj, the reward is the same. The conditions remain the same for giving zakat. It is only when it comes to salat that men have infused something out of the ordinary, something which the Prophet did not approve of. There are many Hadiths of the Prophet asking men not to stop women from going to mosques, or instructing women that the best place for them to offer salat in a mosque is behind men—the best place for a man is in the front row, whereas for a woman it is in the last row. It was gender division, not gender injustice. Yet the way things have taken place in our society, men, at least in the Indian subcontinent, have decided that the best place for women to offer prayers is not in the last row of the congregation in a mosque, but outside the mosque, in the innermost chamber of their houses!

Incidentally, the reason for women to be in the last rows had nothing to do with women's status, but with men's biological weakness. Prayer in Islam, besides being a spiritually uplifting act, is also a physical action involving resting on the knees and going down in prostration. In other words, what in modern terms involves a compromising position; when a person prostrates in prayer, his nose and forehead touch the ground as do his palm and feet, while the back is in a raised position. Hence to safeguard a woman from a man's unwanted gaze, it was thought best that women stand behind men. They still prayed in the same hall on the same floor, not in another room. Noted author Kamala Das, who embraced Islam in the autumn of her life, puts it aptly, 'When a woman kneels behind an imam, she is unlikely to yield to temptation but if a woman is leading the prayers men kneeling behind might look at her haunches, at her curves. Why give them such a chance?'[1]

This modern-day exclusion of women from the prayer space stems from a patriarchal mindset where men are supposed to decide and women are supposed to follow. According to this mindset, good believing men decide with kindness and good believing women obey without question. It goes against the letter and spirit of the Quran, particularly, verse 36 of Surah Ahzab that states,

> And it is not befitting for a believing man or a believing woman, when Allah and His Messenger have decided an affair (for them),

[1] Available at: https://www.thehindu.com/thehindu/mag/2005/05/01/stories/2005050100020400.html

> that they should (after that) claim any say in their affair; and whoso is rebellious to Allah and His Messenger, he verily goeth astray in error manifest.

Rather than women who wish to pray in a mosque going astray, it is the men who prevent them from doing so who are guilty of going astray.

Also, through instances from the life of the Prophet, Muslim men and women have been given examples of what to do and what to avoid. While the Quran asks both men and women to establish prayer, observe fast, give charity, etc., the Prophet is known to have said that the best man is the one who is the best to his wife. And as a mother, the Prophet gave women thrice the rights of the father. Thus, the first right on a child is that of his mother and second and third right too, whereas the man has only 25 per cent right.

No wife of the Prophet ever changed her name, ranging from the forty-year-old twice-widowed Khadijah, who was the richest businessperson of her era, to the nine-year-old Ayesha. They always retained their maiden names. Khadijah was always Khadijah bint Khuwaylid and Ayesha was always Ayesha Siddiqa. Neither of them ever became Khadijah Muhammad or Ayesha Muhammad. Even though they were married to the Prophet, their distinct identities remained intact. They were never regarded as Mrs Muhammad, but always as individuals or mothers of the faithful. In fact, a vast number of Hadiths have come down to us through the narration by Ayesha. Similarly, Khadijah not only stood by the Prophet like a rock, but also gave the entire earnings from her business to the Prophet for the spread of Islam. It is pertinent to recall that when the first revelation came to Prophet Muhammad through angel Jibrail, Muhammad started to sweat from head to toe. Shivering, he went to his wife Khadijah who not only covered him in a blanket, but also believed him when he told her about the visit of the angel and assured him that Allah will not allow his life to go waste as he was a truthful man, always helpful to others. She was the first person to believe the word of the Prophet. The year Khadijah died, as also the Prophet's uncle Talib, he called it the Year of Sorrow. After she had passed away, he remained in touch with her near and dear ones, often sending them gifts in remembrance of his wife.

As for Ayesha, she virtually grew up in the house of the Prophet. She used to accompany him as part of the caravan. Once, the Prophet and she were going along with the Prophet's companions in a caravan. The Prophet slowed down, allowing the caravan to proceed ahead of him. As Ayesha and he were left behind, he challenged his wife to a race. Ayesha was game. She was young, probably in the spring of her life. She defeated her husband in the race. Later, the two joined the caravan.

The Prophet was not done though. He waited for a second chance. It did not come his way soon, but when it did, he made the most of it. Once again, the Prophet, accompanied by his wife, was going in a caravan across the Arab desert. Once again, he slowed down, letting his companions move ahead. Once more, he challenged Ayesha to a race. She was sporting too. The two had another race. This time she lost and the Prophet exhaled, 'Now, we are equal!' Such was his relationship with the women in his life. Such was the importance the Prophet gave to his wives. Now compare this with the actions of the average Muslim man in the subcontinent: Men decide and women acquiesce. It starts with the *nikahnama* and goes on to almost every aspect of their relationship, culminating in the mosques becoming the monopoly of men.

At the time of marriage, hardly any terms and conditions are written down in the *nikahnama*. Terms, such as the stipulation that the marriage should not end with the promulgation of talaq-e-biddat or instant triple talaq and that the man should not take a second wife without the written permission of his first wife, were often present in the nikahs solemnised in medieval India. Today, they have all but disappeared. It is a right conferred upon women by Islam. It is a right taken away by men. Just as they have done with prayers in mosques, at times deliberately, but more so out of sheer ignorance of the dictates of the Quran.

Most Muslim men, and indeed women, do not know the rights and duties conferred upon them by the Quran. A vast majority of people do not know Arabic, so they read the Quran without understanding it, only to get rewarded in the hereafter. Not surprisingly, here is forgotten in this quest for hereafter. Additionally, the maulanas who are often called upon to teach a child the Quran are themselves usually unaware of the contents of the Quran. In their younger days, they would have learnt the Quran by heart without understanding a verse of it. They follow the same method in teaching. As a result, a man might have completed the first reading of this entire book by teenage, but is unaware of any of its teachings.

Thus, as an adult when he steps out for prayer on Friday, or on any other day for that matter, he sees only men going for prayer. He imbibes the same values: men go out for salat, while women pray at home! It is a fallacy that finds support from no verse of the Quran. In fact, when the muezzin gives the azan, the call for prayer, he invites everybody without any discrimination on the basis of gender. When he pronounces, 'Hayya allas Salah, Hayya alal Falah' meaning, 'Come for prayer, come for success', he invites both the genders to the path of success. Men, being men, often close this path of success for women in the subcontinent. Men, or at least some of them, accept the invitation and proceed to the mosque for establishing prayer while women are left behind, rather denied the right to accept the invitation.

In fact, the Quran talks of *falah* (success) around forty times. Right at the beginning, through Surah Baqarah's verses 3 to 5, it is said,

> ... who believe in the unseen, establish prayer, and spend out of what We have provided for them, and who believe in what has been revealed to you (O Muhammad), and what was revealed before you, and of the Hereafter they are certain (in faith). Those

> are upon (right) guidance from their Lord, and it is those who are successful.

Further, the Prophet said, 'Adhere to the righteousness and you will be successful. And know that the best of your deeds is prayer.'

The Quran says it. The Prophet said it. The clerics in the subcontinent do not always understand Arabic. The common people are seldom taught the language in school, and women continue to be deprived of their right, their path to success. Women pay the price for the ignorance of men.

Women are told that the best prayer for them should be conducted in the innermost chamber of their houses. It is an oft-quoted Hadith wherein a lady Umm Humayd, caught in a troubled marriage with a husband who would not give her any freedom, told the Prophet, 'O Messenger of Allah, I love to pray with you.' To which he said,

> I know that you love to pray with me, but praying in your house is better for you than praying in your courtyard, and praying in your courtyard is better for you than praying in the mosque of your people, and praying in the mosque of your people is better for you than praying in my mosque.

It is important to remember that even at that time there were men who asked the Prophet to prohibit women from coming to mosques, but the Prophet declined their requests.

In the specific case of Umm Humayd, he did not say 'the prayer of women is better in their rooms'. Instead, he directly told her, 'Your prayer in your room is better for you.' He didn't say that Allah would reward women more if they prayed in the innermost room of their residence, or that Allah would reward Umm Humayd for praying in the innermost room of her house. He simply said it was better for her. It could be interpreted as the Prophet's attempt to bring peace in her marital life. It is important to reiterate that in Islam one is even allowed to speak a half-truth if it can bring estranged spouses together.

In any case, this was for a specific case where a woman was often faced with distraction from her husband, so she was advised to go to the inner chamber where he would not be present. More importantly, even as the Prophet advised her to stay indoors for her prayer, he did say, 'praying in the mosque of your people is better than praying in my mosque.' In other words, he suggested to the woman to opt for a local mosque, which would entail less travel time and keep her away from her husband for a shorter period of time. It is important to remember that Umm Humayd's husband Abu Humaid Al-Saedi was from the family of Bani Saedah, a branch of Medina's Al-Khazraj tribe. The clan lived just outside Medina at that time, pretty much isolated from Al Masjid an Nabawi. The Al-Khazraj tribe had its own mosque and council. Taking these ground realities into consideration, the Prophet intended to bring about a rapprochement between the spouses, as her husband was unhappy with the fact that his wife had to travel so much to reach the Prophet's Mosque five times a day. His suggestion to Umm Humayd was specific, and not general in nature. In no way did he tell all women to stay away from his mosque, or any mosque for that matter.

This is the only Hadith that is quoted by the clerics in India and the neighbouring countries. What is not as often stated is the Prophet's advice to men: 'Prevent not the servant of Allah, who are females, from entering the Mosque.' Or another Hadith wherein the Prophet is reported to have said that the best place for a prayer for men is in the first row while for women it is in the last row. With the Prophet clearly speaking in terms of rows of worshipers, it does not need a genius to understand that he did not bar the entry of women from mosques. Men and women prayed in the same hall during the time of the Prophet. He did not ask for separate rooms for women. Nor did he shield the women with a cloth screen or any other barricade. He did not stand for gender-specific mosques, and anybody, as long as he/she was decently attired, was permitted to join the congregation. All he expected the women to do was to cover themselves in loose garments from head to foot, and avoid using perfumes that might attract men towards them. Similarly, no man was allowed in shorts; men always had to keep themselves covered from the waist to the end of the knees. Also, numerous instances have been reported of a large congregation of worshipers where the Prophet was leading the prayer. On such occasions, he would choose shorter verses from the Quran keeping in mind that among the worshipers would be old men, who may not be strong enough to stand for long, and women accompanied by small children. Besides, in the Prophet's Mosque, women would often come to pray and even to interact with him and participate in discussions. The Prophet never excluded women from his deliberations. During the signing of the famous Treaty of Hudaybiyyah, when men did not agree to forgo hajj because of the pressure from the pagans, he consulted Umm Salama who advised him to perform the rituals but indicated that they would not be performing the pilgrimage. The Prophet went ahead with her advice. Similarly, during the time of Abu Bakr, the first caliph, when the Quran's master copy was put together—until then people used to only memorise the Quran—the first copy was kept not with the caliph or any of his companions, but with Lady Hafsa. The first copy of the Quran, as we have today, was left with a lady and not with a man! The same book asks both men and women to establish prayer. It is another matter that many men in the subcontinent pick and choose things as per their convenience, thereby ignoring the message of the book that asks humanity to enter completely into faith.

Do treat your women well and be kind to them for they are your partners and committed helpers.

—Prophet Muhammad in his Last Sermon

CHAPTER 2

Makkah's Al-Masjid al-Haram: Men and Women Together in the Sacred Space

On the ninth day of hajj in 632 AD, Prophet Muhammad gave a charter for women's rights for all times to come. Delivered on a Friday in the Uranah valley of Mount Arafat, the Prophet's Khutba Hajjatul-Wida or the Last Sermon was attended by over a hundred thousand men and women in Makkah.

In his sermon, the Prophet outlined what is universally regarded as the charter of human rights, highlighting the Quran's focus on justice for all, irrespective of race, gender, caste or creed, and on equality to transcend the barriers of region or race.

Against the backdrop of the circumstances prevalent at the time of his birth—where women could be captured in war, bought or sold, were denied the right to inheritance, education, conducting matrimonial alliances or were killed at birth—the Prophet's words were revolutionary. He did not give women just the right to life; he gave them a reason to hope for better, more egalitarian and just days ahead. In his Last Sermon, the Prophet declared that just as men had rights over women, women too had unequivocal rights over men.

Their Own Space: Women coming out after offering prayers at Corniche mosque in Jeddah

Much like the Quran says through a part of verse 228 of Surah Baqarah, 'And women shall have rights similar to the rights against them; But men have a degree (of advantage) over them. And Allah is All Mighty, All Wise.'

At the completion of hajj, pilgrimage to Makkah involving among other things, circumambulation of the Kaaba, the Prophet said in his final address,

> O People it is true that you have certain rights with regard to your women but they also have rights over you. Remember that you have taken them as your wives only under Allah's trust and with His permission. If they abide by your right then to them belongs the right to be fed and clothed in kindness. Do treat your women well and be kind to them for they are your partners and committed helpers. And it is your right that they do not make friends with any one of whom you do not approve, as well never to be unchaste.

The Prophet, in the same address, called women 'partners of men'. It is this sentiment that stays with a man on a hajj pilgrimage to Makkah.

It is here that his message is implemented in letter and spirit—men and women are partners to each other.

The hajj is one of the five pillars of Islam, and it is a sacred duty of every Muslim to undertake it once in his or her lifetime unless prevented by ill health or inadequate finance. The Kaaba signifies the unity of Muslims across the world. The cycle that starts with the establishment of five daily prayers in the neighbourhood mosque, and proceeds to the Friday prayers in the largest mosque in the area, culminates with a pilgrimage to Al-Masjid al-Haram, the largest mosque in the world.

During the daily prayers, one is supposed to interact with the fellow residents of the area. During the Friday prayers, one has to mingle with the residents of the city. During hajj, one meets believers from all corners of the world—the hajj attracts over 2 million pilgrims every year.

The pilgrimage is a beautiful advertisement for gender justice. Men and women, young or old, gather from across the world and perform all rituals of faith together. Women are not exempted or prohibited from any ritual, be it the tawaf—circling the Kaaba in an anti-clock fashion seven times—the sacrifice of an animal, spending a night at Muzdalifah or casting stones at the three pillars in a

Beautiful from the Inside: A view of the Corniche mosque in Jeddah

United against Evil: Men and women stone the Devil as part of Hajj pilgrimage

symbolic stoning of evil. Both men and women do the same thing, and are said to reap the same reward for the effort.

Whether from the Indian subcontinent, West Asia, Africa or the US, men and women perform prayers at the same place at the same time. For instance, besides circling the Kaaba, they offer two *rakat*s (cycles) at Maqam-e-Ibrahim. There is a huge rush at the spot, and often one finds oneself standing in prayer next to the opposite gender. In fact, during tawaf too, men and women are together. It is quite common to find women holding on to the arm of their husbands during tawaf, as there is a perpetual danger of missing a step or stumbling because of the huge rush of people from behind.

Women from the Indian subcontinent and those from South-East Asia are the most vulnerable due to physiological reasons—in comparison to women from Africa or Europe, women from these regions are shorter and not as stout. Interestingly, nobody objects to husbands and wives holding each other's hand or even pulling the other person with force here, which is quite contrary to the scene in

No Gender Division: Men and women perform rituals together during Hajj pilgrimage

India where women, on a rare appearance in a mosque, are totally avoided.

At Hateem too, where the faithful believe no prayer goes unanswered at the spot, husbands and wives try and help each other enter it. Same for Hajr-e-Aswad, a black stone believed to have been brought from paradise by angel Jibrail.

According to one of the more accepted narratives behind the stone, when Prophet Ibrahim and his son Ismail were building the House of Worship, they fell short by a stone. So, they had to look for a stone to fit in one of the four walls. Prophet Ibrahim asked his son to go and look for a stone that would fit in the space that was available. The son went but could not find a suitable piece of stone. Upon his return, he was surprised that his father had already placed a stone in the available space. Upon asking, Prophet Ibrahim told him that it was brought to him by angel Jibrail. Today, men and women vie with each other just to touch it; husbands and wives physically help each other to reach Hajr-e-Aswad.

Together in Umrah: The author with his daughter during Umrah pilgrimage in Makkah

Not just at Maqam-e-Ibrahim or Hajr-e-Aswad, the hajj itself is a tribute to the efforts of the wife of Prophet Ibrahim, Hajra. As part of the major or minor pilgrimage, hajj and umrah, the faithful visit the Safa and Marwa, once two hillocks. It is believed that Prophet Ibrahim, on following orders of Allah, left his wife Hajra and infant son Ismail in the desert of Makkah, near the Kaaba, as he went out for business. Initially, Hajra had enough to eat and drink. Once the provisions ran out, and she was unable to feed her son, she frantically looked for water to quench the thirst of her child. Seven times, she ran between the hills of Safa and Marwa, but all seven times she failed to find water. That's when Ismail started scraping the land with his foot and suddenly water started gushing out! All this in a barren desert with no visible source or sign of water. Overwhelmed, Hajra tried to take the water in her palm and enclose it in the sand and stones. Thus came about the famous Zamzam well—Zamzam literally means 'stop flowing', denoting Hajra's effort to keep the water for her child. To this day, pilgrims run or walk briskly between Safa and Marwa, denoting Hajra's frantic search for water. They carry with them the Zamzam water, too.

Over the centuries, the Zamzam well has continued to satiate the thirst of billions of people. Initially, it was surrounded by a simple fence of stone. Some believe that in the early days it had two cisterns, one for drinking and the other for ablution. Periodically given a facelift, its last major restoration work was done a little more than a hundred years ago, during the reign of Sultan Abdul Hamid, an Ottoman ruler.

Today, men and women drink from the same source and wax eloquent about its healing qualities. Men and women are each other's partners, just as the Prophet has instructed. However, this is only one part of the Prophet's Last Sermon that is followed here at Al-Masjid al-Haram. The Prophet also gave a responsibility, in the same sermon, to the assembled people to pass on the message to those who were not there, and each succeeding generation taking the message forward.

The Prophet said, 'All those who listen to me shall pass on my words to others and those to others again; and may the last

Hand in Hand: Men and women help each other during the strenuous pilgrimage in Makkah

ones understand my words better than those who listen to me directly.'

Unfortunately, in this inter-generation passing of information, the essence has not always been retained by all. Like the people who quote a Hadith attributed to the Prophet's wife Ayesha wherein she is supposed to have said, 'If the Messenger of Allah had seen what new things the women have introduced (in their way of life) he would have definitely prevented them from going to the mosque, as the women of Banu Isra'il were prevented.' What they fail to see is that her words did not amount to rejection of the rule. She acted in response to an emergent case at her time. She did not mean cancelling the permissibility or even recommendation of it. When asked about preventing women from frequenting the mosque, the Imam of Medina, Imam Malik, who lived just a few decades after the Prophet's wife, said, '(Women) should not be prevented from going out to the Mosques.'

All this is forgotten by men in the subcontinent. They are the men who deny women the right to space in mosques in the Indian subcontinent despite praying with them at Al-Masjid al-Haram and Al-Masjid al-Nabawi in Medina. When they go for hajj, they are happy to take their mothers, wives, sisters and daughters along. They perform the same rituals and offer their prayers in their respective spaces inside the premises. They help each other move forward in tawaf, too. It is when they go back home to, for example, Delhi, Mumbai, Chennai or Kolkata, or even Lahore, Karachi and Dhaka, that the patriarchal male order raises its head. Then, cultural relativity is considered paramount and the Prophet's dictate of women being partners of men becomes secondary. The men who pray in the presence of thousands of women at Makkah ask their women to pray at home on their return. Not once does it strike them that by this same logic, women in hajj or umrah should be praying in their hotel rooms, and not circumambulating the Kaaba!

The ironies can be self-consuming. However, it is sufficient to remember that one of the traits of Allah whom the believers beseech on pilgrimage is justice. He is Adil, one who does justice. He loves adl (justice). Denying women their rightful place in mosques everywhere is an injustice men cannot explain away.

One *salah* offered in my masjid is superior to one thousand *salahs* offered in other masjids except Al-Masjid al-Haram.

—Prophet Muhammad

CHAPTER 3

The Perspective from Medina

Tall, strong and a strict disciplinarian, Caliph Umar was all set to lead the prayers at Al-Masjid al-Nabawi. As was his wont, soon after the Takbir, prayer call, he insisted on all the rows of worshippers being absolutely straight. As the main imam of the Prophet's Mosque, he would often pass by the rows of people standing for prayer and say, 'Stand in straight lines.' With his personality—he was a wrestler, an able horse rider and a rare well-educated man of his era—when he commanded, he was instantly obeyed. The men stood in neat rows, and close to him stood two of his faithful companions Abdullah bin Abbas and Amr bin Maimun. Behind men, stood many women. Among them was Atiqa, Umar's wife.

The fact that she stood there was nothing but a small victory for Atiqa. A noted poet, she was among the first ones to migrate to Medina with the Prophet and his companions. She loved to pray at the Prophet's Mosque—the Prophet had permitted women to do so, and Atiqa was the happiest. After her marriage to Umar, however, she discovered that he was not exactly pleased with her decision to pray at the Prophet's Mosque. Yet he was aware of the Prophet's instruction on the subject, and could not have gone against the decision. He didn't say anything. Atiqa would often ask him to go to the mosque with her. But Umar kept quiet. His silence was a mark of displeasure at her going to the mosque. Atiqa though never stopped asking for his permission to go to the mosque and insisted on going unless he specifically asked her not to.

The author during Umrah pilgrimage

Umar used to remain quiet. He knew he could not prohibit a thing the Prophet had permitted. Atiqa took his silence as approval and continued to offer her prayers at the Prophet's Mosque.

As it turned out, Caliph Umar would lead the prayers after assuming caliphate in 634 AD, and his wife would stand behind him where the rows of men ended. One day when Abdullah bin Abbas and Amr bin Maimun stood behind Umar as he began the Fajr prayer, Caliph Umar was stabbed by a Persian–Christian man named Abu Lulu'ah. It caused instant commotion with the caliph collapsing almost immediately. He held the hand of Abdur Rahman bin Auf and asked him to lead the prayer as he himself was bleeding profusely. Abdur Rahman led a short prayer. However, the attacker was not done yet. He was carrying a double-edged knife and he stabbed whomsoever he found in his path. He ended up stabbing thirteen worshippers—of whom seven later attained martyrdom—before he was overpowered by a man who threw his cloak over him. Realising he was captured by the worshippers, he killed himself. Caliph Umar, meanwhile, was helped by his companions to his home. Realising that he was seriously wounded and may not live for long, he appointed a six-member council to select the next caliph, Uthman ibn Affan. Caliph Umar breathed his last three days later, but before that he sent a messenger to Ayesha, the wife of the Prophet, expressing his wish to be buried in the compound of Al-Masjid al-Nabawi alongside the beloved Prophet and the first caliph, Abu Bakr. The Prophet's wife respected his wish saying, 'I had the idea of having this place for myself, but today I prefer Umar to myself.' Thus, he was laid to rest close to where he used to lead the prayers.

Grief-stricken Atiqa, who had seen her husband being stabbed in front of her in the mosque, composed an elegy for him. She wrote,

> Eye! let thy tears and weeping be abundant
> and weary not—over the noble chief.
> Death hath afflicted me in the fall of a horseman
> Distinguished in the day of battle...
> Compassionate to those closest, tough against his enemies,
> someone to trust in times of bad fortune and answering,
> whenever he gave his word, his deeds did not belie his word,
> swift to good deeds, and not with a frown.

Indeed, Umar was as good as her words. Having embraced the faith at the age of thirty-nine, after reading Surah Taha's verse, 'Indeed, I am Allah. There is no deity except Me, so worship Me and establish prayer for My remembrance,' his bravery, gallantry and rare talent enabled the faithful to cross many a hurdle. The Prophet gave him the title of al-Farooq, meaning the one who can distinguish between the right and the wrong. Incidentally, he was responsible for Muslims being able to pray in public. Until he joined the fray, others were not confident of praying in public. With the stature of Umar, nobody confronted the believers.

Atiqa's presence at the time of Umar being stabbed silences all who insist that a woman's best prayer is at home. The Prophet did not stop women. Umar, as a caliph and chief imam of Al-Masjid al-Nabawi, did not prevent them either. Imagine what the Prophet would have said at this denial of the right to women—more so, at a time when faith was completed for all times to come with the completion of the revelation of the Quran.

Umar was not around anymore, but Atiqa continued to pray at Al-Masjid al-Nabawi. In fact, when she married Zubayr ibn al-Awam after Umar's departure, she set a precondition. It was stipulated in the marriage contract that he would not beat her and she would not be prevented from visiting the Prophet's Mosque at will. Zubayr agreed. Later, however, he regretted his decision to permit her to attend the prayer by *jamaat* in the mosque. He tried to discourage her, whereupon Atiqa said, 'Are you so jealous that you want me to forsake a place where I have prayed with the Prophet, Abu Bakr and Umar?' With her persistence, Atiqa not only found a way for herself but also set an example for all the succeeding generations. Today, the Prophet's Mosque is visited by more than 23 million pilgrims each year. A little less than 40 per cent of them are women.

In fact, if one goes to Al-Masjid al-Nabawi today, there is a clear and warm acceptance of women. They have a number of halls reserved for them and take part in five daily prayers apart from Taraweeh, Eid and funeral prayers. More importantly, the halls reserved for women are changed regularly, thus giving both genders a chance to experience the complete premises. When the Prophet had initially built the mosque, he used to stand against a tree trunk for support while giving his sermon. The mosque itself came into existence in a unique way. When the faithful migrated to Medina, the Prophet came here on a camel. As he entered the city, the rich and powerful men lined up to welcome him, each hoping he would alight at his home. The Prophet though moved on, telling them, 'This camel is commanded by Allah; wherever it stops, that will be my home.' The reins of the camel were let loose. The camel moved on until it reached the site of the present mosque and knelt down. That is when the Prophet got down too and inquired from those around about the piece of land and its owners. He was told that the land belonged to two orphans, Suhail and Sahl. The Prophet purchased the land from the brothers and had it cleared of all its vegetation. He decided to build a mosque here and he himself took part in its construction. The city that was till then being called Yathrib now came to be known as Madinah-tun-Nabi (City of the Prophet). He, however, did not build any majestic mosque, but simply a functional place for prayer and for the faithful to assemble in. Its roof was made of tree trunks and branches of the date palm. In one corner, a place was left for the poorest companions of the Prophet to stay. The mosque had multiple doors: Bab al-Rahman or the Door of Mercy, Bab-e-Jibrail or the Door of Jibrail and Bab al-Nisa, the Door of Women. Again, the fact that right from its early days, the mosque had a door reserved for women proves that the Prophet never prohibited women from coming to the mosques, and any modern-day prohibition is a *biddat*. The mosque has undergone innumerable revamps, the first being merely seven years

In Their Own Right: Women at the Prophet's mosque in Medina

after it was built, when the height of the roof was raised to counter the oppressive heat. Later, during the time of the caliphs, particularly, Umar and Uthman, improvements were recorded as the mosque's columns were changed to stone, replacing the initial tree trunks. Then, during the times of the Umayyads and the Abbasid rulers, the mosque was significantly expanded. Even the last resting place of the Prophet was incorporated into the mosque, and so were the residences of his family. The Ottomans gave the mosque a significant facelift. Today, it is one of the largest mosques in the world—it takes a good five minutes from the gates to reach the complex proper, where each hall is covered with expensive rugs, chandeliers, water coolers and everything that the faithful might need during their prayer. Nothing distinguishes a hall for men from the hall for women except a little signage at the entrance. Both the genders visit the last resting place of the Prophet and those of the caliphs, and offer their salutations from behind a lattice screen and move on. Many men and women then take their place in their respective rows and stand shoulder to shoulder to offer *salah*, feeling happy and content to have prayed here. It is believed that a prayer here is better than a thousand prayers elsewhere. As the Prophet had said, 'One *salah* offered in my masjid is superior to one thousand *salah*s offered in other masjids except Al-Masjid al-Haram.'

Yes, indeed. And it is the same for men and women, just as it was when Atiqa prayed in the mosque behind the likes of Abdullah bin Abbas and Amr bin Maimun.

Do not prevent your women from going to the mosque if they ask your permission.

—Prophet Muhammad

CHAPTER 4

The Scene in India: Mosque as a No-Woman Zone

Around fifty times, the Quran asks men and women to establish prayer, rather than merely offering prayer. A prayer is established in a congregation when we stand shoulder to shoulder in submission to the Almighty. A man praying alone is not regarded as having done his duty unless the circumstances so dictate. These exceptional circumstances could range from the complete absence of mosques in the city to a serious illness, or even being held up due to some urgent matter elsewhere. But at all normal times, in places where a mosque is available and the sound of azan, the prayer call, can be heard, a person is supposed to go to the mosque and establish prayer in a congregation. Back in the times of the Prophet, a visually impaired man had once asked him for permission to pray at home rather than coming to the mosque five times a day. There were no-well paved roads and streetlights then, and the possibility of an animal attacking a man could not be ruled out. The Prophet, initially, allowed the man to pray at home but asked him if he could hear the azan at his home. The man replied in the affirmative. Upon this, the Prophet asked him to join the congregation at the mosque. The Prophet laid so much importance on praying together with the brethren that even a visually challenged man was not exempted. Praying by *jamaat* (collective), five times a day, was compulsory and not an optional activity.

In fact, it was advised that if somebody was getting late for the salat (Islamic prayer), and reached the mosque after the other devotees had completed their prayer, the latecomer should team up with a man similarly placed and offer prayer in a small group, which can be as small as just two men, rather than merely offering his own individual prayer.

This is fine. But what about women? The Quran asks them to establish prayer too. The Prophet also ruled in favour of women who wished to come to the mosque for prayer. Once a woman was coming to the mosque at the time of Fajr prayers and on the way she was criminally assaulted by a man. The man was later apprehended and brought before the Prophet. The Prophet instructed that he be executed. He did not ask the woman to stay home. She continued to come to the mosque. This action of the Prophet puts to rest all apprehensions of those who fear for the security of women, and, hence, recommend that they should stay home for their daily prayers.

The sacred book does not discriminate between men and women. The reward for every act of piety is the same for both genders. So is the punishment for sin. If a man is expected to perform hajj or give zakat, if he has the means, the same is expected of a woman. Similarly, if a man is supposed to be flogged for zina or improper sexual relations outside marriage, the woman too is to receive the same punishment. Also, on matters of consultations women have equal rights. Incidentally, once Caliph Umar called for a meeting of the community at the Prophet's Mosque. Men were seated on one side and women on the other. Then, he announced his intention to fix a mahr (dower) amount for women at the time of marriage. While men listened in silence, a lady objected, stating that something like mahr was not fixed by the Prophet. So, he could not do so either. The caliph agreed with her saying, 'The woman is correct, I am wrong.'

Taking this equality a step further, how do women establish prayer today in the way they are expected and permitted to do by the Quran? How do they congregate for prayer in most mosques across India? Well, they don't. Unless, of course, one is referring to a few mosques run by Jamaat-e-Islami Hind or those founded by the Ahl-e-Hadith sect and a few other mosques in the bigger cities and towns. In the vast majority of mosques in India—the estimates go up to 95 per cent—women cannot establish prayer on a regular basis in a mosque. While a handful of mosques do 'permit' women to come inside and pray in solitude, most do not. Incidentally, 'permit' is not the right expression, no matter what sundry clerics say. It is a woman's right to go to a mosque. Islam confers that right. It safeguards the right of women to go to mosques and pray there, but it does not make it compulsory for them, unlike men. They are offered a choice, unlike men. They are exempted, but not prohibited from attendance in mosques; particularly women with infants or small children. The Prophet himself instructed men not to stop women from going to the mosque if they so wished.

However, in India mosques are a male monopoly, a virtual no-woman zone. Right from conception to completion, a mosque is designed to facilitate men devotees; women do not figure in the scheme of things. For most men who design mosques in modern India, or those who run the management committees of various mosques—no mosque is known to have women members on their management committees—it is inconceivable to plan a mosque with special provisions for women. Mosques are places for men, men and more men. Practically, women are not allowed. The entrance, the wudu khana, the toilet, the shoe rack, the prayer hall, the shelf for keeping the Quran, everything is by men and for men. If perchance a woman comes, she is made to feel completely alien, as if she has stumbled into the wrong place.

Sample this: most mosques have two facilities pretty much near the entrance gate. The first is a wudu khana or the place of ablution. In this section, tap water is readily available to wash one's hands, face and feet as part of the wudu essential to offer salat. Most wudu khanas keep a stool, either a plastic one or a cemented, fixed variety, to enable men to sit as they wash themselves. The stools, the water pipeline, everything is designed keeping in mind the physical structure of an average Indian man. The distance between the stool and the tap also is designed to enable a man with average to large arms to access the water easily.

There is no separate wudu khana for women. So, in a corporate area of any metropolitan city, if a working woman were to go from her office to the nearest mosque to offer prayers, and she is lucky enough to be 'permitted' to do so, she would struggle to do her ablution. In most cases, she would have to do it under the male gaze, despite the fact that the prayer place is a strict gender-segregation zone. Most men in a sacred space would lower their gaze, as advised in the Surah Noor verse that says, 'Say to the believing men that they should lower their gaze and guard their shyness (and looks) and protect themselves and their privacy (from illicit sex): That will make for greater purity for them: Verily, Allah is familiar with all that they do.' However, the possibility of some not able to 'lower their gaze' cannot be denied. The performance of wudu itself is considered part of the prayer. Hence, one is strongly advised against talking to fellow devotees while performing ablution.

However, the difficulties for a woman worshipper neither begin nor end with the wudu khana. They begin right at the entry point. Most mosques do not have a separate entry for men and women, as is strongly advised. A woman who braves the odds and comes to a mosque to offer prayers in a congregation often has to wait for the menfolk to trickle in before finding her own space to enter, as there is no separate gate for women to use. It is at this first step that a woman has to guard herself against an unwelcome touch or an avoidable physical contact with the opposite gender. Having cleared the first hurdle, the next one lies just a few steps ahead. In India, many men prefer to use the mosque's washroom rather than any public convenience to attend to nature's call. Hence, most mosques in non-residential areas construct multiple flush toilets for men; some even offer the convenience of the western commode. No problem with that, but again no thought is given to women. It does not strike men who maintain the mosques or those who construct them in the first place that women too can come to mosques and can have bodily requirements as well. Most mosques do not have a separate toilet for women. It is assumed that a handful of women who might come to pray would have attended to their bodily exigencies in the privacy of their homes or offices. No thought is spared for women travellers who might just come to a mosque on their way to a railway station or airport! Of course, no such elementary challenges await men in a mosque! Everything is provided for them.

If a woman is lucky and is able to attend to her needs at any place but a mosque, she faces the next hurdle: the wudu khana. Yet again, there is no separate wudu khana or ablution corner for women. It is here that a handful of women devotees have to either wait for all men, even those who come after them, to finish their business before entering the section. Else, as some intrepid ones do, they have to look for a secluded corner in the wudu khana and pretend that nobody is looking as they clean their hands, feet and face for salat. Incidentally, it is here that one cannot help but recall what the Quran says about keeping the gaze lowered.

Through Surah Noor [verse 30], the Quran asks men to keep their gaze low, thereby emphasising modesty. It is only the next verse that asks women to do the same. In the wudu khanas of most mosques across India, most women have no alternative but to believe that every man who comes to pray at the mosque will follow this dictate of the Quran.

The ablution is completed, but the challenges continue. As a woman devotee enters the mosque, she finds there is no prayer chamber or hall designated for women. Most mosques do not even have a small room reserved for them to establish prayer. Most men, out of respect, turn their gaze away when a woman enters a mosque. However, it does not help matters for a first-time woman visitor to the mosque. No signboards are put up to enable a woman to look for her prayer space. Ultimately, the woman is left to fend for herself. In the absence of a designated prayer hall or room, women often end up standing behind a pillar or in a semi-lit corner for their prayer, as most of them are self-conscious.

Yet, standing in prayer after finding a corner, or even a designated place in a handful of mosques, is not easy. If a woman works at a place where hijab or head cover is not allowed, or if she is not carrying one with her on that particular day, the mosque provides zero facilities in this regard. It is in stark contrast to the provision for men. Almost all mosques keep a few skullcaps for men who do not carry a prayer cap in their pocket and do not wish to offer prayer without covering their heads. Yet no thought is spared for a woman who wishes to offer prayer but has not brought along a scarf or stole to cover her head completely.

If a woman is able to overcome this hurdle too, or comes well prepared and dressed for the congregation, her struggle does not necessarily end there. As a woman, she would find herself in some remote, less-visited corner of the mosque, an area that provides her better seclusion for prayer and keeps her away from the gaze of men. Incidentally, Prophet Muhammad had said that the best prayer for a man is in the first *saff* (row), and the best prayer for a woman is in the last *saff*. He emphasised this gender segregation to avoid the often unwelcome gaze of men. It was done as much to safeguard a man's prayer for the fear of his mind diverting to other things at the time of prayer, as to protect women. He, however, did not ask for separate prayer halls or chambers for both genders, but just separate rows for worshippers, men being in front and women at the back.

Thus, in a mosque in modern India, as a devout Muslim woman, she has ticked all the boxes of what is expected of her: attended to her toilet needs, performed her wudu, found a prayer corner and stood away from the gaze of men. Yet, as she finds, often it is in this part that the imam is not clearly audible. She may have walked many a metre or driven a few miles for her prayer, surmounted all the odds of a patriarchal society to reach the prayer place, yet here she suffers due to men's lack of attention to detail. The audio system is barely audible here. Hence, even as the imam recites verses from the Quran, women occasionally have to strain their ears to follow each word clearly—something like this led to a protest from women in South Africa. These women walked out of their section to pray in an unused section of the mosque where they could listen to the recitation clearly.

The prayer is over. Has the mission been accomplished too? Well, not really. If a woman wants to follow up her prayer with a recitation of the Quran, she would better carry her copy of the Quran, for, inside the mosque, the Quran is usually not available to women devotees. All the shelves used for keeping the copies of the Quran are in front of the first row of worshippers. And women being in the rear row or a stand in a separate hall are the farthest from the Quran. A woman either has to walk across rows and rows of men—and most do not—or else, confine herself to reading from her mobile, if she is carrying one. The same lack of thought is exhibited when it comes to rosaries. These too are stacked for the men in front and none for the women at the back. Unless, of course, women start going to a rare mosque that has a special zone for them to pray in.

The prayer done and a chapter of the Quran read, yet a woman's challenge is not quite over. While the Prophet is said to have waited a few minutes after completion of the prayer, enabling women to file out first, no such thought is given in the Indian mosques. Again, as a woman, she has to wait for men to amble out of the mosque before she can find her way. Often, men decide to chat with each other after prayer and unwittingly block the passage to the sole entry and exit of the mosque. A devout woman has no alternative but to wait for men to clear the premises and then look for her shoes or sandals that she might have stuffed under some rack or a safe corner—you see, there is no provision for women to remove their sandals and place them securely outside. As a result, some even prefer to carry a little polythene bag or an old newspaper to put their footwear in before they enter the prayer hall.

For a woman in an average mosque in India, struggle marks every step of the way. Mosques are, essentially, an all-male zone, a place for male congregation, a place where a woman is neither mentioned nor thought of. Men stand shoulder to shoulder, ankle to ankle. They submit themselves to the Almighty together. But what about women? Ask an average devotee and he would reply, 'Isn't the best prayer for a woman at her home? And there too in an inside room?' The selective use of faith continues to haunt Muslim women in the Indian subcontinent. Forgotten is the fact that for a couple of centuries after the departure of Prophet Muhammad, women continued to come to the masjid. It is after that the Islamic jurists of the time began to disapprove of women praying in mosques, and 'because of the degenerating social values, father and husband, apprehended that their womenfolk might not, by some lapse of conduct, disgrace them.'[1] This mindset, giving men the ownership over women's actions, and any supposed lapse on their part to bring dishonour to them, stemmed from the deep patriarchal value system that was well entrenched by then. It was against this discriminatory system that the Prophet preached against female infanticide and gave women the right to pursue

[1] Salam, Ziya. 2018. 'Rebel with a Cause'. Available at: https://frontline.thehindu.com/other/obituary/rebel-with-a-cause/article10085035.ece (accessed on 25 April 2019).

education, own property, conduct matrimonial alliances, etc. To men he advised not to stop women from coming to mosques. And a man guilty of criminal misconduct with a woman was executed on the Prophet's orders, but the woman was not prevented from coming to the mosque. It is time for menfolk to remember that.

O you who have believed, when (the adhan) is called for the prayer on the day of Jumuah (Friday), then proceed to the remembrance of Allah and leave trade. That is better for you, if you only knew.

—Surah Jumuah [verse 9], The Quran

CHAPTER 5

The Scene on Fridays and Taraweeh

Every Thursday, mosques across the country undergo a hurried cleaning exercise. The carpets are vacuum cleaned and the webs on the walls are removed. The wudu khana is washed and cleaned. It is almost like the mosques are awaiting some important guests soon. Turns out, it is in preparation for the weekly Friday prayers when the number of devotees goes up drastically. If on a normal working day mosques register nominal attendance during the afternoon prayers, it is exactly the opposite on a Friday. This is the day when the Quran specifically instructs the faithful to leave everything aside and proceed to the mosque. The belief is, the sooner one reaches for the prayer, the greater is the reward. The mosques that attract only around 50 worshippers on any given day play host to more than 500 people on a Friday. Incidentally, it is on this day that a sermon, khutbah, precedes the actual prayer. In this sermon, the community is given advice on emerging socioreligious issues, besides an address on Islamic history. It is a sermon well taken. Across the country, you will find thousands of men sitting in rows and rows inside the mosques and listening with rapt attention to every word spoken by the imam. It is time to assimilate the message and practice the advice given.

All that is fine and, in some ways, practical to tackle the emerging challenges too. But around 50 per cent of the Muslim society is excluded from the Friday sermon. While the Prophet encouraged women to attend the Friday service apart from the special prayers on Eid, most mosques exclude women through their action. With hundreds of men assembling in each mosque, women who wish to offer Friday prayers with fellow sisters have their task cut out. Yet again, there is no provision for their ablution and none for their prayer section. As a consequence, in the mind of the common man, Friday is the day when Muslim men gather in large numbers to offer prayers, while women cool their heels at home. Or at best, pray as they usually do: inside their home and all by themselves. It strikes nobody that if men who offer salat by *jamaat* are said to get twenty-seven times the reward of a prayer offered in private, what do women get? How do they earn that reward? And unlike everyday prayers, the Friday service cannot be performed at home. Yet, there is nothing more than a whisper of protest here. Women continue to regard Friday as the day when the menfolk in the family dress up in their crisp kurta pyjama, don a skullcap, apply attar (fragrance) and head for the mosque. Friday, once again, reiterates that mosques in India are a no-go zone for women.

Things are repeated continuously in the month of Ramadan, the holiest month when each little act of goodness begets much greater reward than rest of the year. In the run-up to Ramadan, most mosques are given a fresh coat of paint. The carpets are either thoroughly cleaned or replaced. The air-conditioners are serviced, the water coolers are checked and the audio system is double checked. After all, Ramadan is the time when even those who do not offer five daily prayers come to the mosque to pray with their brothers. Many mosques are illuminated too.

Every evening, the effort seems worth it. A little more than an hour after the fast is broken with the setting of the sun, the faithful start heading to the mosques for Taraweeh, the special prayers in Ramadan. Thousands of men finish work early in their offices to reach the local mosque in time for the Taraweeh prayers. Old men, who otherwise struggle to walk, muster up the strength to attend the service. Hardly a surprise, there is not even an inch of space available in any of the mosques as the faithful listen to the imam reciting the Quran. In fact, many mosques even have worshippers spilling over to the road. In most mosques across North India, the imam rushes through the chapters of the holy book in an attempt to complete the recitation of the Quran in a few days, whereas in Kashmir and large parts of South India, the recitation is more nuanced, much less hurried. However, across the country, it is only in a handful of mosques that the imam explains the Quranic verses in the local language as well. Usually, it is only the Arabic recitation. No surprise then that a large majority of imams do not themselves practise what they recite—the Quran asks both men and women to establish prayer, but society fails to listen.

Even as thousands of men gather for Taraweeh, it is not unusual to see food stalls come up outside many mosques with stall owners waiting for the faithful to finish their prayers before coming to the stalls to satiate themselves. Once the prayer is over, the scene shifts to the food stalls. Once again, it is just men and more men. Women are, to use a cliché, conspicuous by their absence.

Hardly any mosque, even in Ramadan, makes provisions for women to offer special prayers. Most do not even have a women's section. Some do admit, almost grudgingly, a handful of women who might come to pray, considering nobody likes to give prayers in Ramadan a miss. However, this is doled out as a concession. There is little likelihood of women standing shoulder to shoulder, ankle to ankle with each other to establish prayers even in the month of Ramadan, when each prayer offered is said to get at least seventy times the reward of a prayer in the other eleven months of the year. As a consequence, it is not unusual every evening post-iftar to find women praying all by themselves at home, while the menfolk go to the mosques. Men fulfil what is required of them by faith, but what about women?

This has been going on for more than a hundred years. In fact, ever since the British arrived, mosques and madrasas have been reduced to areas of male monopoly. Such is the indoctrination of long years that most women themselves have either bought the male narrative that mosques are for men only or that the best prayer for a woman is the one offered in the inner room of her house! This is the same old interpretation and the same old denial of rights to women. Forgotten in the din of social instruction is the message of the Quran, the words of Surah Jumuah where the faithful, men and women, are asked to leave everything aside when it is the time for prayer.

> Visit the graves for they will remind you of death.
> —Prophet Muhammad, Sahih Muslim, 259

Women in Funeral Prayers

It is said if a funeral prayer is attended by at least forty people, the departed man or woman goes to Jannah (paradise). Most people in and around Al-Masjid al-Haram in Makkah (even Al-Masjid al-Nabawi in Medina) bring the bodies of their dear departed for the funeral prayer here, knowing there is never a shortage of worshippers at this place. After almost every prayer in Al-Masjid al-Haram, there is a quick announcement in Arabic through which people are asked to stay on for a funeral prayer. There is hardly any daily prayer that is not succeeded by a quick funeral prayer, where the faithful stand shoulder to shoulder, men as well as women. The prayer itself does not take more than a couple of minutes. However, in those couple of minutes, there is a strong statement issued on gender parity in Islam. Yes, after the imam makes an announcement to ask the faithful to stay on for a funeral prayer, usually of a complete stranger, both men and women stay on and participate in the final prayer of the departed.

In the Indian subcontinent though, this is never ever done. It is quite common for the leading mosques in the country to host funeral prayers. It is not rare for an imam to ask the worshippers to stay on after the Friday prayers for namaz-e-janaza (funeral prayers).

Again, the menfolk usually stay on for a few minutes for the final prayer of the departed. And women? There are hardly any women in the mosque! And among those who do attend the prayer service open to them in a handful of mosques, most leave before the funeral prayers. It is inculcated into their minds that funeral prayers can only be offered by men. That many of these women would have performed hajj or umrah, and thus may have availed a first-hand invitation extended by an imam there for a funeral prayer fails to awaken them to their rights. It has been so for centuries. Women do not participate in funeral prayers here. But the same women, when they go to Saudi Arabia for pilgrimage, attend funeral prayers. Yet when they are at home, in India, Bangladesh or Pakistan, they hardly ever even ask for permission to attend the funeral prayers of somebody who they might have loved intensely, or somebody who may have influenced their life in a major way. Always, even for the last prayer of their parents, siblings or spouse, women never take part in the funeral prayers. This is amazing, considering when a child is born in a Muslim household the first thing that is done is to say the azan in the ear of the newborn. The funeral prayer is said to be the one that follows the azan, life itself being nothing more than an interregnum. It symbolises the fleeting nature of life. It is the same for both men and women.

Yet, women are never seen at a funeral prayer. Not even when the departed is a fellow woman. In such a case, women help with giving a ceremonial bath to the departed. They wrap the body in a shroud and apply attar. Some recite the Quran next to the body. Soon after, the body is taken to a mosque or cemetery, where the final prayers are offered. Women are conspicuous by their absence.

Under these circumstances, noted human rights activist and lawyer Asma Jahangir helped carve out a piece of history with her death. After she breathed her last in February 2018, scores of women assembled for her funeral prayer in Lahore. Most locals could only recall the funeral of Mohammed Ali Jinnah, the founder of Pakistan, when women had attended the last prayer. Otherwise, it was a piece of history that was created with the participation of women in Asma's funeral. According to *Frontline*,[1]

> The media publicised the picture of women standing in a *saff* (row formed for prayer), defiance writ large on their faces, next to men behind the body. In a country that is used to seeing only men attending burials, the image epitomised many things that Asma Jahangir stood for. The revolt against tradition did not end with the funeral prayer in Lahore. Asma Jahangir was buried not in a traditional cemetery but in her family farmhouse in a manner that is fitting for one who lived her life according to her own set of principles.

In *Dawn*,[2] Rimmel Mohydin, South Asia Campaigner for Amnesty International, wrote,

> Rumours spread that Asma's funeral would be led by her sister and long-time activist Hina Jilani. That only women would shoulder her shroud. Every woman I know held her head a little higher when they heard of this possibility ... I told this to my colleague on the way to the funeral. He responded, 'It's never going to happen.'

It did not. But what did happen was indeed the rarest of the rare spectacles. Women, in hundreds, attended the funeral prayers, probably for the first time in the living memory of most participants. Rimmel wrote,

> A woman next to me asked the women around her to make space for a line. Then she raised her voice slightly to spread the instruction. Soon, she and three other women were shouting over

---

[1] Salam, Ziya. 2018. 'Rebel with a Cause'. Available at: https://frontline.thehindu.com/other/obituary/rebel-with-a-cause/article10085035.ece (accessed on 25 April 2019).

[2] Mohydin, R. 2018. 'The Silence at Gaddafi during Asma's Funeral was a Reminder of What Losing a Champion Sounds Like'. Available at: https://www.dawn.com/news/1389379 (accessed on 25 April 2019).

> the men, demanding more room. More and more people began to shuffle in the space, stepping to their right, stepping to their left, moving forward, moving backwards. Asma's daughter Munizae asked the men to cooperate. Rows upon rows formed. Silence fell over us again. The Imam began his prayer. I suddenly realised, this was the first time I had offered a prayer that was led by a male Imam. It did not feel out of place. It might have, had I been the only woman there.

Interestingly, this participation of women in funeral prayers was a daring first step towards breaking tradition in Pakistan. That it came barely two weeks after Jamida had become the first woman to lead mixed gender prayers in India meant that the spirit of change was beginning to blow across the subcontinent.

However, challenges remain. Two days after the funeral, *Pakistan Today* reported that a lawyer had filed an application seeking the registration of an FIR against the women who took part in the funeral prayers. The report noted,

> A lawyer has filed an application with the Gulberg Police Station seeking the registration of a case under Section 295-A against the participants of prominent human rights lawyer Asma Jahangir's funeral. After Asma Jahangir's abrupt death due to a cardiac arrest, many of her female comrades, colleagues and relatives joined the prayers at Gaddafi Stadium, which was led by Syed Haider Farooq Maududi, son of Jamaat-e-Islami (JI) founder Syed Abu'l Al'a Maududi, in the front row. The application filed by Advocate Amanullah seeks the registration of a case against Farooq Haider Maududi, Muneeza Jahangir, Saleema Jahangir (daughters of Asma Jahangir), and around 100 more people who attended the funeral.

Mercifully, the clerics refrained from calling the participation of women in funeral prayers un-Islamic, objecting only to women standing in the first row. Fair enough. The Prophet too said that the best prayer for a woman was in the last row.

Hussain is from me. And I am from Hussain.

—Prophet Muhammad

CHAPTER 6

The Shia Narrative

After every Sunni mosque in India, you will find another Sunni mosque. And another. Then, after maybe after around twenty mosques of various sects and subsects of Sunnis you will find a mosque for Shias—the two communities have started to pray together in some mosques and have also started offering the Eid prayer together over the past five years or so. In some Shia mosques, Sunnis too offer prayers and vice versa. This is usually borne out of logistical reasons. If a Sunni mosque is not close by, a Sunni man may prefer to pray at a Shia mosque rather than offering prayers in isolation at home. The Shias do the same. For instance, at Jama Masjid, New Delhi, it is common to find Shia men standing with their Sunni brothers in prayer; the only distinguishing characteristic being the way Sunnis cross their hands across their chest, while the Shias do not do that.

On first appearance, a Shia mosque is not necessarily different from a Sunni mosque unless, of course, an *imambara* is attached to the mosque. The *imambara* is a sociocultural centre usually adjacent to a Shia mosque. Here, men and women gather during the period of Muharram for collective mourning. The imam addresses them, often reiterating the age-old tale of Karbala. The story, down the ages, would have been repeated thousands of times. Yet, it never fails to move the faithful to tears. No Sunni mosque has an *imambara* attached to it or any sociocultural centre for free exchange of views, or even education of the Quran and Hadith. A Sunni mosque is just a place for prayer. A Shia mosque, partly because they are much fewer, doubles up as a community space. Also, while the Sunnis prostrate both directly on the ground and on the rug or mat, if the mosque has a wall-to-wall carpeting, it is different with Shias. Under no circumstances do Shias prostrate on the rug. It always has to be a clay tablet. This tablet is made of clay brought from Karbala or Najaf in Iraq. In some cases where the clay tablet is not available, the prostration is on a piece of natural wood. But it is never on a man-made thing. So, all the expensive carpets are ruled out.

The Shia mosques in India are better equipped to deal with exigencies of life and death. Most Sunni mosques confine themselves to lending a wooden slab or low station table for bathing the departed. In some cases, they provide a byre too. Among the Shias, there are complete arrangements for bathing the dead in their mosques. Many *imambaras* too have proper bathrooms for the dead. These include women too. And this is what distinguishes them from the Sunni mosques. There are complete arrangements for women's last rites, including the ceremonial bath, covering in a shroud, applying fragrance, etc. As only women can bathe dead women, arrangements are in place to use the services of women in the vicinity, or even trained women can be recruited from a distance. There is no such provision in the Sunni mosques for women. Almost all Sunni women are given their last ceremonial ghusl (ritual washing of the body) at their home. Also, considering very few Sunni mosques make arrangements for the dead, things are not very different for men either.

This is for the dead. When alive, Sunni and Shia men team up to keep women out of the mosques in the country. Most Shia mosques have no provision for women's *jamaat*. No mosque in the big cities, such as Mumbai or Chennai, keeps a row at the back reserved for women. In fact, the denial of this space to pray in the mosque appears more pronounced among the Shias. While more of the Sunni mosques are beginning to keep a little corner for women, albeit grudgingly, often as an afterthought, things are slightly worse in the Shia mosques. Here, the best a woman can hope to do is drop in at a moment of her need and offer her individual prayer. For instance, if a woman is in her office and it is time for prayer, she can go to a mosque as and when she has time and offer her prayers privately, but not in a congregation. Doing this she does not necessarily face any trouble and no quizzical looks are given nor is she made to feel unwanted. But the concept of women standing in a *saff* to offer prayers behind an imam does not arise. Like with Sunnis, Shia men go to the mosque, offer prayers collectively and leave their women to pray at home individually. The mosques offer zero facilities to women for performing ablution, for attending to their body needs and the like. Men also remind women that the best prayer for them is at home. The imams, who command a lot of respect and following in the Shia community, seldom broach the subject of women's right to enter the mosques. When it comes to women's space in the mosques, there seems to be a conspiracy of silence. Also, they do not give a translation of the Friday sermon in the local Indian language very often. Again, much like the Sunni men of India, who have no problems in praying in a mosque with women—both have their respective rows or rooms—when away to West Asia or the US, the Shia men do the same. When they visit Iran or even historic sites, such as Najaf or Karbala in Iraq, they often see women frequenting the mosques. They find that mosques keep women in their mind at the planning stage itself. The Shia men of India are happy to pray with women in the Shia world abroad. When they come back to India, the patriarchal forces reassert themselves and the religious dictates take a backseat. And women resume their prayers in the privacy of their homes, just as men would like them to. The only exception being a little trip to an *imambara*, if there is one, like in Lucknow or Hyderabad or Noida. There, women get a little section to themselves. Again, such is the indoctrination of women that some of them despite being in an *imambara* and hearing the call for prayer, prefer to offer their prayers in their individual space rather than standing shoulder to shoulder with their sisters in faith. Like a Sunni woman would do at home after hearing the azan, a Shia woman occasionally does the same in an *imambara* or even a mosque, preferring to offer her prayer individually rather than joining the congregation. More is the pity.

They do not, honestly try to understand the Quran, or are their hearts locked up by them?

—Surah Muhammad [verse 24]

CHAPTER 7

From the Eyes of Scholars

A little less than sixty years ago, renowned Islamic scholars Maulana Abu Ala Maududi and Dr Israr Ahmed were locked in an intense debate on the way ahead for Jamaat-e-Islami, which the former had founded in pre-Partition India. Maududi had then been preaching about restoring the Islamic order with the caliph at the helm of affairs; the caliph in turn drawing his energy and guidance from the Quran and Sunnah, a body of literature that prescribes the practices of the Prophet. Under this order, there was no scope for *riba* (interest), as Islam stood for interest-free economy. Riba, in Islam, amounts to fleecing the poor to feed the rich. A person who devours interest and does not desist from it is not just condemned but regarded as one at war with the Almighty. Indeed, the Quran, through Surah Baqarah [verse 279] states, 'And if you do not, then be informed of a war (against you) from Allah and His Messenger. But if you repent, you may have your principal—(thus) you do no wrong, nor are you wronged.'

Inevitably, Maududi believed that a democratic country swearing by the Constitution passed under the leadership of Dr B.R. Ambedkar stood at dissonance with the message of Allah. As a believer, he felt, it was imperative to strive to attain a sociopolitical-economic order based on the message of the Quran. He set about achieving the aim earnestly. However, India's Independence with its attendant partition put a spanner in the path. Maududi soon realised that to be a part of the new order, the Jamaat-e-Islami will have to have its own bank account; thereby becoming part of interest-driven capitalist economy, if only out of sheer compulsion. On the subject of participation in electoral democracy too, he realised that the community needed to send its representatives to the Parliament to have any realistic chance of modulating public discussion towards the direction it strove for.

After his views began to be implemented at the ground level and Jamaat became a part of the political system, Dr Ahmed parted ways with Maududi. He decided to chart a long and lonely path towards a possible restoration of an Islamic sociopolitical-economic order. While Maududi was initially considered a conservative scholar, the ensuing events took him closer to the liberal category, confining Dr Ahmed to the conservative circles.

Even as Maududi shifted his base of operations to Pakistan, the organisation, the Jamaat, he founded in undivided nation started using the tools of democracy to take the message forward in India. Active participation in the electoral process was encouraged, and over a period of time, the Jamaat came to have its own political wing too, all working as per the rights and responsibilities provided by the Constitution of India. Gradually, the Jamaat began to open up. It started its own women's wing and soon made space for women among its mosques across the country, thereby becoming probably the first Muslim body to accommodate women. In contrast to most other mosques that, at best, provided elementary facilities to women, the Jamaat actually reserved an entire corridor at its Delhi headquarters' mosque as well as separate floors in many mosques in Kerala. While some mosques did have a corridor earmarked for women worshippers, at other places, due to paucity of available land, the basement or the first floor was reserved for women. Though it was not exactly in consonance with the prevalent practice during the time of the Prophet, it at least gave women an opportunity to pray with their sisters five times a day and the hope to earn a reward similar to the men. In fact, it is not unusual to hear the Jamaat's chief ask all women to come to the Jamaat mosque on Eid, including women who might be menstruating, and hence are exempted from prayer. He would advise them to take part in *dua* at the end of Eid salat. This was a revolutionary message in a country where a vast section still believes that menstruating women should not be allowed inside a mosque or prayer hall.

Though confined, by and large, to Delhi and Kerala, the Jamaat model of mosques shone splendidly in comparison to mosques maintained by some other bodies, notably the Jamiat Ulema-e-Hind or those under the influence of Tablighi Jamaat. While the Jamiat admits women worshippers, it makes absolutely no provisions for them. The mosques are not women friendly—no gate is earmarked for them and no section, hall or room is reserved for them. If at all a woman comes in of her own will, she usually ends up offering prayer by herself, rather than in a group, thereby defeating the purpose of going to a mosque. The story stays the same, whether at their headquarters in Deoband in Uttar Pradesh or the main mosque at ITO in New Delhi. Women do not exist in the conception, planning or implementation at the Jamiat mosques.

While the Jamiat at least looks the other way on the issue of women's entry into mosques for prayers, thereby giving a tacit nod to their presence in its mosques, the Tablighi Jamaat is more robust in its opposition. Without screaming from rooftops, its volunteers, wherever they are in sizable numbers, reduce mosques to an all-male domain. Incidentally, most mosques in the Hindi-speaking belt of the country fall under the influence of the Tablighi Jamaat, where twice a day a small chapter of *Fazail-e-Amal*, a book that is attributed to its founder Muhammad Ilyas Kandhlawi, is read out. The book is a collection of Hadiths, some authentic and some not so, and some anecdotes. It has a particular appeal for first generation learners and those whose exposure to literature seldom goes beyond what is trotted out at the Tablighi gatherings. Every day after Fajr and Asar prayers, a volunteer of the Tablighi Jamaat stands up in a mosque to address the faithful. He invites them for 'deen ki baat' (conversation of faith). It does not strike them that prayer itself is a conversation between the worshipper and the Almighty. It is caused, at least partly, due to the lack of understanding of the message of the Quran. The Tablighi Jamaat leaves the study of the Quran and its interpretation to the scholars. What or who is a scholar is never clearly outlined. With such vague state of affairs, the Tablighi Jamaat members concentrate not on exploring the meaning of the Quran, but on the Hadith related to everyday rituals. With even men being denied the right to understand the Quran or explore its meaning, the exclusion of women from the mosques under the control of the Tablighi Jamaat is both inevitable and unavoidable.

Any mention of women's *saff* (row) inevitably attracts an endless reiteration of the Hadith related to women's best prayer being in the innermost chamber of their houses! What is forgotten is the Prophet's message wherein he asked the faithful to take the message of the Quran forward, even if all they knew was just one verse of the book! No negotiation, dialogue or debate works here. Women, for them, have to be at home. Their primary purpose in life is child rearing and other domestic responsibilities, and there is no space for them in the mosques. The best they can hope to do to answer the azan, if they hear one, from the seclusion of their homes, is to pick up their prayer mat and pray in the innermost room of their house. That the Quran asks women, as also men, to establish prayer rather than merely offering prayer in private does not register with many volunteers of the Tablighi Jamaat, who dismiss any attempt to make space for women as nothing but fitna (mischief).

On the subject of exclusion of women from the mosques, the body finds surprising support from Dr Ahmed. In most of his lectures, Dr Ahmed, born in Hissar in pre-Independence India, encouraged the faithful to explore the meaning of the Quran and see the text against the context. In fact, his hour-long lectures on various chapters of the Quran are hugely popular online. However, in the case of women going to mosques for prayer, he often repeated the Hadith related to Umm Humayd's query. In *Religious Obligations of Women* he wrote,

> Women are exempted from the congregational prayers and encouraged to pray at home. At home, it is preferred that they pray in a room instead of the lawn. If the room happens to have a small chamber within it, then the chamber is preferred over the room. Exceptional has been the case of the congregational Friday and *Eid* prayers. Women were encouraged by the Prophet to attend these two prayers. This was due to the fact that no communication media and other means of propagation (books, magazines or audio/visual facilities) were available in those days. The sermons of Friday and *Eid* prayers were the sole source of education and information for them. However, these are two exceptions and the overriding rule is that it is better for ladies to offer their prayers privately in their homes rather than at public places.

He, however, conceded that women were merely discouraged and not prohibited from going to the mosques. He argued,

> Islam discourages unnecessary intermingling of genders and determines separate spheres of activity for them. In this context, we can easily understand why a woman's prayer is best in the most secluded part of the house, and why her presence is discouraged in the mosque (though not forbidden).

His views echo those of Hanafi jurists. Incidentally, at least 80 per cent of the Indian Muslims are followers of Imam Abu Hanifa. This is a conservative sect, one that regards instant triple talaq valid and does not approve of women's entry into the mosques. They argue that during the time of the Prophet the women had a unique opportunity of praying behind the Messenger of Allah. It is an act which is not possible today. Women then used to observe all requirements of the law of Islam, including covering themselves fully. Hence, the Prophet did not prohibit them from the mosques. The Hanafis also claim that Caliph Umar felt that the concession given to women to visit the mosques was misused by some women. He felt that some women were no longer observing purdah to the desired extent.

Hence, according to Hanafi jurists, the caliph gave a verdict that women should no longer attend the Friday prayers at the Prophet's Mosque. His decision is said to have been accepted by the other companions. The Hanafi jurists often recall a saying of Ayesha, the Prophet's wife, wherein she said, 'If the Messenger of Allah was alive to see what women are doing now, he would surely have prevented them from attending the prayers in the Mosque just as the women of Banu Isra'il were prevented.' The Hanafi scholars take this a step further and say that if she had witnessed what women are involved in these days, she would have been more extreme in her views and prevented them from entering the mosques. 'The women in her time were not involved in even one portion of a thousand of what women are up to these days,' they contend.

The arguments were, however, settled by the noted Islamic scholar of the 20th century, Mufti Abdul Dayam, who wrote in *Tajreed Bukhari Sharif*, 'Women can participate in jamaat (congregation).' Quoting Anas, a companion of the Prophet, Mufti Abdul Dayam wrote,

> My grandmother Malika invited the Prophet to a dinner. He enjoyed the hospitality, then stated, 'Get up. I will lead the prayer for you.' There was at home a well-worn out mat now turned black. I sprinkled water on it, and stood for prayer. The Prophet stood in front to lead the prayer. An orphan boy and I stood behind him. Behind us old women stood. The Prophet led us in two rakaats [cycle] and went back.

He also wrote in the same book, quoting Umm Salama, 'When the Prophet would conclude prayer with a "salaam" then women would get up and leave. And the Prophet would wait for a little time before getting up.' He also repeated the oft-quoted Hadith of Ayesha stating, 'The Prophet used to pray Fajr at the Mosque and believing women used to go there in their cloaks. And after the prayer, the women would head home. Nobody recognised them.' With this recollection, he laid to rest all arguments that women were prevented from going to the mosque by the Prophet, or even the caliphs.

Incidentally, Islamic scholars of Indian or Pakistani origin are on the same page on this subject. Contemporary Islamic scholars and preachers Yasir Qadhi and Nouman Ali Khan have made no secret of the fact that women were permitted to pray in the mosques by the Prophet. In fact, speaking on *Bayyinah TV*, Ali Khan, in one of his lectures, talked of a Hadith seldom found elsewhere.

> Once women came to the Prophet. They complained that when they came for Fajr (dawn) prayers, they often soiled their garments because of the sewage on the way. In the dark, they were not able to see properly to avoid sewage. Hence, they wanted to be allowed to pray home. The Prophet heard them out, but did not ask them to stay home. Rather he said, 'You come. The dry soil you walk on (after the segment with sewage) will clean the clothes of filth.'

Khan, thereby, contended that women enjoyed no exemption from public congregation in those days, not even for the prayer completed before the first ray of the sun.

He also gave a fresh interpretation to Umm Humayd's case. In one of his lectures he stated,

> The woman was caught in a troubled marriage. Her husband was super jealous of her. He used to poke her as she prayed. The woman complained to the Prophet who asked her husband the reason for his behaviour. The husband said he was angry because his wife had stolen his surahs. In other words, he used to lead the prayers until his wife memorised the verses, and started praying on her own. He could not bear to live without her at all. The Prophet told the woman to pray at home so as to save her marriage. And at home, if her husband still disturbed her, she should go to the closet to pray.

Khan also gave a new twist to the oft-repeated message of Caliph Umar seeking to prevent his wife from going out to pray at the Prophet's mosque. He said,

> The part of the world I come from, Pakistan, and by extension, India and Bangladesh, women are not allowed in the masjid. More than half the population cannot even pray there, and they call it an Islamic country! I was told stories of Hazrat Umar throwing stones at women coming to pray at mosque. Let me reiterate, women get equal reward for going to mosque as men. If men get 27 times reward for going to mosque, women get the same. Women during the time of the Prophet used to walk in the middle of the night to pray at the Prophet's mosque. As for Umar, he never stopped his wife Atiqa from praying at the Prophet's mosque. Pertinent to recall that he was the Imam of the mosque at that time, and could have used any means at his disposal to do so. Still he never prevented her from going to mosque even though he was concerned for her safety at night. So, he devised a pretty intelligent plan. As she went to pray, he threw a couple of stone[s] in her path. She got scared and ran home. Problem solved. Three days later, she found out it was him, and she started coming to masjid again! This is one of the versions I heard growing up. The truth is he never stopped his wife from praying at the mosque as he knew the Prophet's instruction on the subject.

That his wife continued to go to the mosque is borne out of the fact that she was with him in the congregation when he was stabbed. It is also narrated by Salim ibn Abdullah ibn Umar (grandson of Umar) that his father Abdullah ibn Umar (son of Umar) said, 'I heard the Prophet saying, "Do not stop your women from the mosques when they ask your permission to go there." His son Bilal said to him, "By Allah we will certainly stop them".' Upon this Abdullah turned and abused him. Later, Salim recalled, 'I have never heard him abusing anyone like that.'

Qadhi took the argument a step further. He talked about the practice of *itikaf*, in which a person retreats to a mosque in the last ten days of Ramadan and concentrates only on worship. In the subcontinent, the practice, again, is carried on only by men, many of whom take ten days off from work and retire to a mosque. Women, in the subcontinent, however, are encouraged to do *itikaf* at home. Hardly any mosque makes provisions for them. Qadhi stated,

> It is Hanafi sect that allows women to do itikaf at home. The Quran is explicit that itikaf is done only in masjid. Umm Salama and other wives of the Prophet wished to do itikaf. Her house was connected to the mosque. Yet a special tent was set up inside the mosque for her. It clearly demonstrates that itikaf should be done only inside the masjid, be it men or women. Itikaf means to stick to a place, cut yourself from the world. You remain in an area and worship Allah 24 hours a day. In masjid you will be cut off from family, and hence immersed in worship. The same is not possible at home. Many mosques do not allow women to do itikaf for logistical reasons.

From five daily prayers to the Friday prayers to the Eid prayers, on to *itikaf*, and even the funeral prayers, women are denied their due. What is worse, many have even stopped thinking of it as their right. Such is their indoctrination.

Seeking knowledge is a duty upon
every Muslim male and female.

—Prophet Muhammad

CHAPTER 8

Fair and Fine in the US

The Prophet established the mosque as the centre of Islam. It was an inclusive place with men, women and children there not just for five daily prayers, but also for learning, for discussions on the Quran and for consultations on every day affairs of life. Even for talks about an impending war or strategising for it. Not just Muslims even non-Muslims came to take part in deliberations. At times, they also brought their problems to the Prophet for amicable settlement. Once the Prophet entered his mosque, he found one group busy discussing the Quran and the other group helping each other with the perfect recitation of the book. On another occasion, he sat in a distant corner of the mosque and observed how a man, who came for prayer, performed ablution and then prayed. Once he was through, the Prophet asked him to repeat his prayer, as he had not performed it the right way.

One is reminded of the original concept of a mosque while looking at the evolution of mosques in the US. Almost every mosque is inclusive, both men and women are welcome. Further, the mosque is indeed the centre of the faithful's life here. From being open to both genders for daily and Friday prayers to special Taraweeh prayers in Ramadan to provisions for learning to read the Quran and reciting it the right way, to learning Arabic and following the commentary of most scholars of repute, the mosques offer it all. While all these facilities are open to men and women,

The Bilal Masjid in the US not only has designated prayer space for women but keeps in mind the special needs of mothers with toddlers and little children

the latter in particular are well taken care of. In the women's section of the mosque, which is usually just behind the men's section, there are facilities for lactating mothers, those with toddlers, those with physical disabilities, like needing a forehead rest due to an inability to prostrate on the ground. Some mosques provide kindergarten or crèche facilities as well, where working women can leave their kids from seven in the morning to four in the evening. This is possible because more women are seen in the mosques during that time. Take for instance, the Muslim Association of Puget Sound (MAPS) Mosque in Redmond, Washington. The mosque has separate rooms for mothers and tiny tots, mothers and infants and mothers with little children. The area is designed in such a way that children can see everything outside from a glass window, while their mothers offer prayers. It keeps children busy, enabling the mothers to offer their prayers in peace and quiet. On the subject of children, the Prophet advised the faithful not to stop children from coming to the mosque. He himself used to indulge his grandchildren Hasan and Husain, who would often climb over him when he knelt in prostration. The Prophet would calmly put them down as he resumed his standing position. Many of the mosques in the US, notably the MAPS or Islamic Center of Redmond (ICOR) or even Bilal Masjid in Oregon, live up to this message of the Prophet.

The MAPS Mosque has a capacity of around 1,500 people, some 10 per cent of whom are women in the Friday prayers. The facility has a barrier between the men's section and the women's, but everybody prays in the same room. The mosque welcomes women in more ways than merely worshippers. It also runs a school from its premises where some 50 women lead the way, teaching sciences, Maths, English, Arts and the Quran to the little ones. A few hours after the school wraps up for the day, there is a family get-together organised to discuss matters of religion and everyday life. The issues could range from the problems faced by immigrants from the Indian subcontinent to the angst faced by those from Jordan, Palestine, Syria and Egypt. Issues of regional or ethnic identity crisis within the fold of Islam are discussed too. The mosque, in fact, provides more facilities to women than men, keeping them involved in the affairs of the place. On weekends, it offers Quran classes in Arabic, English and Urdu, and Hijabista classes for young girls just beginning to wear the hijab or not being confident enough to wear one. The interaction at the gym or over a game of badminton helps break the ice. The girls who start interacting with the peer group over a game of badminton often go on to teach at the mosque, besides attending regular prayers.

The story at most mosques is the same, the facilities provided though vary from opening the doors to women and enabling them to read the Quran in Arabic to those focusing on all aspects of metropolitan life. In Redmond only, the Islamic Center offers facilities directly related with Islam. For instance, it offers Quranic

Women coming out of Bilal Masjid

Tajweed classes for both genders, where students get to learn the root word of the Quran besides the Aalima course, similar to those offered in Islamic seminaries in the subcontinent. The Center runs a preschool also from its premises. Understandably, around 100 women turn up for the Friday prayers here and around 200 to 250 for the special prayers in Ramadan.

The scene is repeated at the Oregon's Bilal Masjid, where women show up daily for prayers and scores of them attend the Friday prayers. The mosque offers complimentary iftar facilities for both men and women. The sermons at this air-conditioned mosque, with ample parking space, are delivered in English, while the Friday khutbah is in Arabic only. The mosque goes beyond being a mere prayer space. It organises charity events, fundraising drives, health camps and book readings as well. The mosque invites foreign Islamic scholars to give special lectures on weekends. The weekend is also the time it has a Sunday school for children, wherein they are taught Islamic history, ideals of faith, ways of living in a cosmopolitan society, etc. The role of women gets more active at the Muslim Community Center of Portland where women, besides offering prayers, also whip up delicacies. The food is for sale at the mosque, much like many mosques in India where commercial food stalls are set up outside the mosque. The difference here is that it is the women worshippers who do business. Equally interesting is the Muslim Education Trust Mosque. The Trust, founded in 1993, is dedicated to the betterment of the society and holds programmes facilitating better interaction between Muslims and non-Muslims. It even celebrates the International Women's Day and conducts Sufi conferences. In short, its well-rounded identity takes the mosque beyond being a place of daily worship. Meanwhile, the Muslim Community Center of Portland gives a facelift to the Indian way of donations for a mosque. In the subcontinent, usually a man asks for funds to repair a mosque or to paint it afresh before Ramadan. In doing so, he usually quotes a Hadith or a verse from the Quran. In Portland, when asking for donations, they repeat a verse from Surah Muzammil, 'Lend unto Allah a goodly loan. Whatever good you shall forward on your behalf you shall find it with Allah,

Beyond Prayer: The Richmond mosque is used for more than just offering prayers by women. Here is a shot of women after a badminton game

The Oregon mosque attracts more women devotees on Fridays

as better and richer in reward.' The mosque also offers lectures by visiting scholars and free books.

These mosques and religious centres, in many ways, are reviving the idea of a mosque as conceived during the time of the Prophet. At that time, women came from far and near to offer prayers behind the Prophet. Many brought their children along. Some came over to discuss their problems, including issues of matrimony, others for guidance and everyday affairs. Some women even gave sermons at the mosque, and many men, including the companions of the Prophet, attended them. Nobody was turned away from any mosque. Everybody was welcome. Just the way it is in the US—where people of different ethnicity use the facilities the mosques offer. A row of worshippers in an average mosque can include people of Indian, Pakistani, Arab, French, British, Albanian or Libyan origin along with African-Americans. It is the same in the women's section.

Yet not everybody is happy, and not everything is happy. There is a section of women in the US clamouring for bigger space in the prayer hall, maybe, even the prime space. They are also asking for positions on the management committees of the mosques. They complain that when they are relegated to a side room or the basement, they are never able to see the imam in prayer. Worse, at times they are not able to listen to his lecture properly due to a faulty audio system. The Muslim Women's Alliance is leading the way, asking for women to be given a prime space in the mosques. The Alliance aims to empower Muslim women to become leaders of the community and beyond. It claims that it is guided by the Islamic ideals stating, 'As individuals we have our own strengths but as a united sisters' alliance, we are even stronger and more capable together.'

Now some women have come up with two women-friendly mosques in Los Angeles (LA). These mosques do not exclude men, but make it amply clear that their primary guests are women. It takes things to the other extreme. While in the subcontinent, even in the mosques with provisions for women, it is made clear that men are the primary worshippers, but in LA, it is made clear that this space is mainly for women. Men are an afterthought. Neither policy of exclusion can be defended in the light of the Quran and Hadith. Much more inclusive has been the approach of Islamic Society of North America (ISNA), which took recourse to the instruction of the Prophet to call for inclusive mosques. The active presence of women in the masjid during the time of the Prophet Muhammad is clearly evidenced in numerous hadiths. A statement of ISNA read,

> Hadith confirm that in the Prophet's masjid women prayed salah regularly, attended Jum'ah prayer, made optional prayer (nawafil), did itikaf in the masjid during Ramadan, and met in the masjid. To help facilitate a healthy environment and avoid fitna (temptation), the Messenger of Allah instructed both men and women to dress properly, lower their gaze and guard their modesty. Women received an additional instruction not to wear perfume when attending the masjid.

O Mary, be devoutly obedient to your Lord and prostrate and bow with those who bow (in prayer).

-Surah Al-e-Imran [verse 43]

CHAPTER 9

The Battle in the UK

The winds of change are blowing ever so gently in Britain. Women, often confined to home, or consigned to small, dimly lit corners of the mosques are beginning to speak up and claim a bit of space for themselves. Till early 2018, nearly every fourth mosque shut its doors on women in Britain. They were all-male zones, where men mingled, prayed, confabulated, and women could not enter, not even for a private prayer. Of the mosques who did open their doors to women, albeit reluctantly, 50 per cent of them treated women as second-class citizens inside the mosques. While outside in offices or public spaces, men and women were treated equally, but inside the mosques, it seemed that women were at the mercy of men; men would decide where women could pray, from where they could enter and exit and how many women could come in. While men got large halls, best carpets, ample ablution area and plenty of religious books to read from, the women's section was an apology of a praying space. Often consigned to the basement or an unused corner of the mosque with a small side entry into the back rows, it seemed that the mosques in Britain regarded women not much better than a fitna.

Women hardly enjoyed any positions of responsibility or authority on various committees of the mosques; most were any way monopolised by men. It was particularly so in the mosques under the influence of the Diaspora, people of Indian-Pakistani-Bangladeshi origin who had made Bradford their home and created a mini subcontinent there. Men had long left the subcontinent, most had been in Britain long enough to get British passports, but they had taken with them the subcontinental tradition of denying women their space in the mosques. Occasionally, when some women did step forward to reclaim their space in the mosques, they were either dubbed feminists under the influence of the West, or told, like their sisters in the subcontinent, that the best prayer for women was at their homes, not in a mosque! That there are 3,20,000 homeless people in the UK, including Muslims, did not dawn on them.

However, a masjid is more than just the place where one does prostrations. It is a community space, where one interacts with neighbours and visitors to the area. It is a place for discussing emerging issues and finding solutions to problems confronting the ummah. Denying women the right to bond with fellow women made little sense, either from the point of view of the Quran or the laws of Britain. Women just had to be admitted in, on equal terms, as equal partners.

In August 2018, the lead was taken by some Scottish women who went from mosque to mosque for equal prayer space and a place on the decision-making bodies. They began by asking for a space in the Friday prayers, where they agreed to spread their own rugs or prayer mats behind men inside the mosque. When they were advised to pray outside, these women went to another mosque, then another. They were either denied their space altogether or told to use the small room or floor reserved for them. As the place usually lacked ventilation or a signified approach, the women protested. The widely respected *The Guardian* reported, 'Many mosques in the UK and elsewhere encourage women to pray at home. Where women's sections exist, they are often small, uninviting and accessed through back entrances. Mosques are traditionally seen as places where men gather for collective prayer and discussion.'[1]

Little wonder, the Scottish Mosques for All campaign got a lot of social media attention and unparalleled support from women, including those from the subcontinent in the summer of 2018. These women asked not just for their own prayer space, but also equal spaces in the mosques as well as positions on the decision-making bodies of the mosques. As reported by *The Guardian*,

> Scottish Mosques for All was set up to highlight the importance of including women in decision-making. More than a quarter of mosques in the UK have no facilities for women and, in the remainder, access is often restricted and the space they are given inadequate. The organisation said: 'It is unfortunate that many mosques fail to provide basic access for Muslim women to use the facility to pray or the quality of the space can often be inadequate and not suitable. It is also unfortunate that many mosques have limited or no women present at mosque trustee or managerial level, either intentionally preventing women from taking up these roles or not sufficiently providing a welcoming atmosphere where women feel comfortable to get involved.'

Women sought to change the status quo. In Bradford, where the presence of the community is unmistakable, the Muslim Women's Council sought to raise funds for a mosque led and governed by women. Though the Council claimed the mosque would be based 'on the principles of openness, inclusivity, social justice and sanctuary', it seemed no different from a mosque monopolised by men, and opened reluctantly to women worshippers. Of course,

---

[1] Sherwood, H. 2018. 'Muslim Women Call for More Equality in Running UK Mosques'. Available at: https://www.theguardian.com/uk-news/2018/aug/18/uk-muslim-women-call-for-more-equality-mosques (accessed on 25 April 2019).

the Council insisted it had nothing against men. The mosque 'will represent what is possible when the potential of girls and women is nurtured, rather than locked away.'

Women's attempts to breach the male frontier in the mosques bore fruit when many men decided to lend their voice and support to their campaign. By October 2018, the Muslim Council of Britain came up with a six months programme to train women to run mosques. Some twenty-odd women enrolled for a six-month long, intensive training programme, where they were to visit some of the best practice mosques of the country, and also avail one-to-one mentoring. That the men were not using this programme as merely a ruse to deflect attention was clear when *The Guardian* reported,

> Few mosques in the UK have women on their trustee or management boards, and men outnumber women on all charity trustee boards by two to one, according to the Charity Commission. The MCB said: 'This lack of diversity is unacceptable and it is essential for the management boards of mosques and third sector organisations in general to reflect the communities that they serve in order to function effectively.' The initiative comes as some Muslim women are demanding equal access to and greater involvement in running mosques.[2]

The paper quoted Andleen Razzaq, a former trustee of Al Manaar Mosque in West London and a facilitator in the dialogue. Razzaq said, 'Muslim women are doing amazing work in the community, but often have no experience of being trustees or on decision-making bodies. We need to have big conversations around the barriers to women. Most are cultural; in Islam, men and women have equal spiritual standing.'

---

[2] Sherwood, H. 2018. 'Muslim Council of Britain to Train Women to Run Mosques'. Available at: https://www.theguardian.com/world/2018/oct/04/muslim-council-of-britain-women-leadership-training (accessed on 25 April 2019).

This is a beginning. A lot more needs to be done, as proved by many male worshippers at an East London mosque who turned away women worshippers, forcing some of them to pray outside the gate of the mosque. *The BBC* reported in December 2018, 'Nineteen percent of Leicester's population in the UK is Muslim, according to the Office of National Statistics. That number is on the rise—as is the number of the city's mosques. But the majority of these mosques offer no space to women.'

It seems that the Open My Mosque initiative, founded in 2015, has some more work to do.

Every innovation is misguidance, and
every (one guilty of) misguidance
will be in the Fire.

—Prophet Muhammad

CHAPTER 10

A New Step in Europe

In Belgium's capital Brussels, all is calm, all is quiet. The Grand Mosque has just hosted the afternoon prayers. A few dozen men and a handful of women attended the service. Most worshippers were immigrants, some coming from the working class segment. This is not surprising in a city where some 70 per cent of the population is brought up by immigrants, mostly people of African origin and a significant percentage of Indians and Pakistanis. Thanks to the immigrants, almost every fourth resident of the city is a follower of Islam. It shows an increase in the number of mosques in the city. The Indo-Pak influences are revealed in the absence of provisions for women. For instance, at the Al Jadid Mosque, women have no ablution corner or a proper space to pray.

On the other hand, we have Masjid Umar Bin Khattab, clearly named after the caliph. Here, women are well taken care of. The mosque provides clean, well-lit prayer space with neat rugs, holy books and scarves. It also provides ablution facilities away from the gaze of men and cloakrooms for women.

As for the Grand Mosque, it follows the Saudi pattern; women are not just admitted, but also provided a place of dignity and solitude to pray. The mosque itself was given to Saudi King Faisal in 1969 on a ninety-nine-year, rent-free lease as a goodwill gesture by Belgian King Baudouin. Over the years, the Saudi influence has grown in the region, leading to calls to cancel the lease. Some locals argue that the Muslims here do not integrate with the larger Belgium society, others counter that they follow the rules of the country and practice their faith in their individual capacity. What it has meant for women though is uninterrupted prayer space. It is something they cannot take for granted at the other mosques.

It is also something women in the neighbouring France are fighting with all their might. The struggle in France goes up a notch; women are not just seeking entry to the main prayer halls in the country, but also permission to pray alongside men in the same row. For long confined to the basement or adjacent rooms, they are now clamouring for space in the main prayer hall of the mosque, some even asking for permission to stand with men. The widely respected *RFI* English reported in January 2019 that more and more French women seek equality in mosques, and not just a piecemeal concession handed out as a dole. Reporting about two Muslim organisations launching projects to create 'inclusive' mosques, where women and men can pray together, it quoted the examples of some women who had initially sought their own prayer space in the mosques before retreating, only to come back with the idea of a mosque to call their own. The *RFI* wrote,[1]

> Kahina Bahloul conducts her prayers at home, in her living room. She decided to stop going to the mosque five years ago after she was refused access to the main prayer room. 'I went to the mosque with a group of male and female friends. It was a religious festival commemorating the birth of the Prophet, so it was very important,' she tells RFI. 'The men were told to go in, but we women were told "cross the road and you'll find a room". It was a garage, in fact. So there I was in this garage. The sound system was terrible and the atmosphere was not at all spiritual. Women were cooking and kids were playing. I was extremely disappointed, shocked even.'

[1] Hird, A. 2019. 'French Muslim Women Push for "Inclusive" Mosque in Paris'. Available at: http://en.rfi.fr/france/20190109-french-muslim-women-push-inclusive-mosque-paris (accessed on 25 April 2019).

Mosques in Belgium are usually women-friendly. While most have a separate floor for women devotees, the Grand Mosque, in particular, attracts more women due to its large prayer space, separate and clear entry and exit

Bahloul now plans to set up the Fatima Mosque, named after the daughter of the Prophet. The mosque will welcome men and women in the same room: men on one side and women on the other, she says.

The *RFI* also reported about her plans to lead the Friday prayers, thereby becoming the first woman imam to lead a mixed gender prayer in a country with around five million Muslims.

> Some schools of Islamic jurisprudence like the Maliki school—the most common in the Maghreb—forbid women imams entirely. Other schools accept women imams, but they're allowed to hold prayers only in front of women, or there's a physical separation in the hall so you can't see the women imam.

Keeping her company in this quest is Eva Janadin, who also wishes to establish a mosque where both genders can pray together, with women as imams. 'We want to draw concrete lessons on how you can lead a spiritual life in today's world, following all the new readings of the Koran, new religious concepts and so on,' she told *RFI*.

In neighbouring Germany, a first of sorts was notched up in 2017 when the Ibn-Rushd-Goethe Mosque saw a prayer led by US-Malaysian woman imam, Ani Zonneveld. She gave her address in German even as men and women stood together, some women with heads covered and others exposed.

AFP, a well-known news agency, reported,

> The new mosque, the 88th in the German capital, is located in a rented room on the third floor of the Protestant Johanniskirche (St. John's Church) building. All Muslims—Sunni or Shia, Alawite or Sufi—are welcome in the mosque named after one of Germany's greatest writers, Johann Wolfgang von Goethe, and 12th century Islamic scholar Ibn Rushd, also known as Averroes.

Yet if Bahloul, Janadin or Zonneveld think they are charting a path far ahead of the time, they have a tough competition from their sisters in Denmark. In Denmark, Sherin Khankan has founded Europe's first women's mosque. The mosque, unlike most across the world, is located on the first floor and is adjacent to a clothes shop, making it pretty anonymous. Called the Mariam Mosque, named after the mother of Prophet Isa, also the only lady to have a Surah of the Quran named after her, the mosque has had women leading the prayers for a couple of years now. On week days, both men and women pray here. Fridays though are reserved only for women. The mosque is actually a very small one, with space only for around 150 women at any given time, but in this limited space, Khankan is carving out a piece of history. Soon, she will have some competition as there are plans afoot to build a women-led mosque in Bradford, UK.

If the plan materialises, these women will be the first in Europe to do so. Asia, however, has had women's mosques for centuries, notably in China, where women have even led the prayers some 600 years ago. Though Khankan and others seeking to lead prayers do not quote a verse of the Quran in their favour, instead they point out that no verse prohibits them to do so.

That may well be the case, but if they insist on exclusion of men from the mosques, as in the case of Mariam Mosque in Copenhagen, they could well be repeating the mistake of the countless men in the subcontinent, men who believe women have no right to be at the mosque. In the garb of gender parity, it could well be another step towards gender isolation.

As for both men and women standing shoulder to shoulder, Khankan and others find no support from the Quran, or the Hadith. The Quran itself does not give the process of prayer. It merely asks the believers to establish prayer at the appointed time. The procedure of prayer comes from the practice of the Prophet. The Prophet always led prayers, where men stood in a row behind him and the women stood behind men in their own row. Each row was exclusive to one gender. The mixed gender *saffs* could well be the innovation the Prophet warned about.

Prophet on one Eid finished his prayer and went straight to the women, gave them a sermon, advised them, reminded them of Allah and ordered them to give charity.

—Sahi Bukhari Hadith

CHAPTER 11

South Africa: A Country Divided

In Ramadan last year, coinciding with May–June 2018, the long shadow of Indian men and their patriarchal mindset enveloped the lives of Muslim women seeking to offer prayers in Johannesburg, South Africa. As women tried to offer prayers in an unused room at the Gold Mosque in Ormonde, men objected, asking them to go back to the small room meant for the women's prayer. The room's speaker was not functioning properly. Unable to hear the voice of the imam from their room, the women came down to the unused room. This led to a debate among men, while the women insisted they were not there out of choice, but they had the right to pray there. They quoted from the Quran and the Hadith. Until finally, they realised their exclusion had more to do with men's insecurities than faith. Nelisiwe Msomi, a Muslim social activist, made an intervention, arguing,

> It is ridiculous really. There is no Islamic basis for restricting the access of women. What we are seeing is Indian men who are imposing their patriarchal culture on women without any basis. This culture is so entrenched in the community that it seems like it is Islamic law. We don't see this in other Muslim communities. We don't see it in the Black Muslim community, or in the Malay Muslim community.

Her viewpoint found resonance with the local *Sunday Times*, which reported, 'The inequality at many Johannesburg and Durban mosques has outraged some Muslim women, who say that not only is there a culture of patriarchy and sexism in the mosques but the conduct is against the teachings of the Qur'an.'[1]

The Sunday Times, in its detailed report, quoted many women activists who insisted they were merely exempted from going to mosque, not prohibited by the Prophet.

> Nabeelah Khan, a follower of the religion, said that during Ramadhan women usually went to mosques on a daily basis to perform the Taraweeh prayer while the Qur'an is being recited. Khan said, 'At every mosque there are separate sections for female and males. The women went to the female facilities first and there wasn't a speaker, so they wouldn't have been able to hear the Qur'an being recited. They wouldn't have been able to perform their Salah (prayer) properly. So they went into the mosque and didn't go into the male section, they went to a room outside there and decided they were going to pray there.'
>
> She added, 'Women have been battling with the inequality for a long time. Why should we not be able to do something to be closer to our Creator just so that men will not be distracted? That's a place of prayer, why are you even looking at a woman in a lustful manner? They now take Qur'an verses and twist it to suit their own agenda.
>
> It doesn't say that we can't go to the mosque; it says we don't have to [but] it's compulsory for men. In the time of our holy prophet women prayed in the mosques alongside men.'

The contention of women about being denied their space in the mosques in Johannesburg and even Durban is supported by well-known

[1] Masweneng, K. 2018. 'We Want to Pray in Mosques Too'. Available at: https://www.timeslive.co.za/news/south-africa/2018-06-06-we-want-to-pray-in-mosques-too-says-a-group-of-muslim-women/ (accessed on 25 April 2019).

activist-imam Muhsin Hendricks, who runs Compassion-Centred Islamic Network, an inclusive centre in Cape Town. The Centre is said to be a network of engaged imams, queer Muslims and allies.

'In Durban and Johannesburg, women [are] not allowed in many mosques due to Deobandi and Tablighi influence. The Indo-Pak influence over the decision making body in a mosque often reduces mosques to men-only zone,' says Hendricks. Incidentally, Deobandi is one of the more followed schools among the Indian Muslims; the Barelvi school—based like Deobandi in Uttar Pradesh—enjoys equal patronage. The Tablighi Jamaat is a Sunni Muslim body of preachers. It was started in 1927 by Muhammad Ilyas Kandhlawi in response to a proselytisation campaign launched by some Hindu bodies in the early 20th century. The body, with a vast network across more than thirty countries, believes in gender segregation, confining women to home. Today, Tablighi Jamaat exercises control over vast tracts of North India, asserting its influence over thousands of mosques; thereby keeping women away from them. The Jamaat regularly sends its volunteers to other countries, including South Africa. Only those get to go to South Africa who would have undertaken at least three trips of four months each within the country. It ensures that men who go abroad would have inculcated the Tablighi Jamaat's ideology.

Interestingly, while the mosques in Durban and Johannesburg either do not permit women to enter the mosques or restrict them to a room designated for the purpose, there are no such limitations in Cape Town. Here, women not only pray freely, at times standing next to men in mixed-gender *jamaat*, but even read the khutbah on Friday. It all started with the visit of the noted preacher Amina Wadud in 1994. Wadud recalled her pre-khutbah talk at the Claremont Main Road Mosque in Cape Town in her book *Inside the Gender Jihad*. In an interview, Wadud recalled,

> In 1994, I was attending a conference in South Africa and I was invited to give a q*utba*, (the Friday sermon) in Cape Town. Both

> those who invited me and I knew that this was a landmark event because it could change the idea of Islamic leadership. From that moment, I spent ten years doing research, in order to better understand how women could become prayer leaders. Over the years, I understood the importance of equality in Islam.[2]

Hendricks adds,

> The mosques in Cape Town are under the Indonesian Sufi influence. They are inclusive. They are open to women. In Ramadan, in Taraweeh, at times there are more women than men in some mosques in Cape Town. They are also engaged in other activities like Tajweed classes or learning Arabic in the evening. Some women also use the mosque for memorising sessions of the Quran. It is the same at our Centre. At our Centre there is no objection from any quarter to the entry of women. Our mosque is not a gay mosque, as erroneously believed. It is an inclusive mosque where everybody is welcome. The men who come here to pray do not object to the presence of women. In some ways, they are looking for social acceptance, and welcome the presence of women.

The local clerics claim mosques are not out of bounds for women. 'Nobody stands at the gate with a placard, "Men only",' they reason. In reality though, women are confined to cramped, dingy and poorly ventilated rooms. At times, even to rooms or buildings adjacent to the mosque, thereby defeating the purpose of coming to a mosque. It is not the mosques that are closed, it is the minds.

It is one such action aimed at keeping women away that drove Noorjan Allie and Shameelah Khan to start a campaign called 'Women of Waqf'. It so happened that women had to drive for a long distance to reach a mosque in Johannesburg that gave them

[2] Meringolo, A. 2013. 'Amina Wadud, Portrait of a Muslim Feminist.' Available at: https://www.resetdoc.org/story/amina-wadud-portrait-of-a-muslim-feminist (accessed on 25 April 2019).

Gender-Neutral Prayers: Men and women snapped together in prostration during a prayer in a Cape Town Mosque. South Africa has a number of women-friendly mosques in Cape Town. The scene in Durban, however, is different due to pronounced exposure to Indian missionaries

proper facilities for Taraweeh. Unable to commute easily after a day-long fast, women decided to pray at the Masjid Siratul Jannah in Ormonde, which was closer to them. They were stopped at the mosque by a man. There was a confrontation. The video of the spat went viral, and there started a debate on the place of women within the African-Muslim community. Hence, the campaign Women of Waqf started. The two activists sought proper space to pray in the mosques, a place where they could listen to the recitation of the Quran and also see the imam. It was not possible if they prayed in a little room separated from the main prayer hall. Women got a little consolation initially, with a slightly better praying space in some mosques or the permission to stand behind men in a gallery in other mosques. Yet, it will not be easy to shake off the Deobandi or Tablighi influence, as Hendricks warns. But then, if Indonesia-Sufi influences can be added, and Indian influences sandpapered away, the future may just be smoother than the past.

Whoever goes out to offer prayers in this mosque (Quba Masjid) will have reward equal to that of an Umrah.

—Prophet Muhammad

CHAPTER 12

Wide Open in West Asia

The first mosque in Islam, the Quba Masjid, was built in Medina in the first year of the Hijri calendar, coinciding with 610 AD. Originally, it was a well surrounded by a village, inhabited by the tribe of Bani Amr bin Auf. It is said the Prophet once visited the home of Bin Auf and built the mosque in the area. The mosque came to be called Quba. The well here came to be known as a blessed place as the Prophet's camel first knelt down here to take a long draught of water after the Prophet's journey. Located barely five kilometres from the Prophet's Mosque, today it is the second-largest mosque in the city.

The mosque had a special place in the heart of the Prophet, who is reported to have said, 'Whoever makes ablutions in this house and offers one prayer therein, will be rewarded the equivalent of one Umrah.' The Prophet himself made it a habit to walk down to the Quba Masjid every Saturday. Sometimes, he would also ride a camel to the mosque. Either way, once there, he would offer two *rakat*s (cycles of prayer) at the mosque. The pilgrims to Makkah and Medina usually halt at the mosque for brief prayers. Inevitably, the mosque experiences an influx of people throughout the year, more so during the hajj times. Men and women both pray here, particularly large gatherings are witnessed at the time of Fajr (dawn) prayers. Beginning with the times of Caliph Uthman, the mosque has been periodically renovated. Today, it is an architectural marvel with four minarets, fifty-six domes and seven main entrances and twelve

Famous Facade: A view of the Dubai mosque from outside. It has ample space for women inside where photography is prohibited

subsidiary ones. It also has a library, a commercial centre and sixty-four toilets for men and thirty-two for women. Thirty-two toilets for women in a single mosque! And still, the clerics in the subcontinent advise women to pray at home!

Impressive as the figures are for Quba, the mosque does not stand in isolation. Be it the mosques from the 7th century or those from the 20th or the 21st century, they all have ample space for women. Often derided for its conservatism—the country permitted women to drive only in 2018—Saudi Arabia has been even-handed when it comes to women's rights in mosques. Be it in proper cities in Dammam, Riyadh or Jeddah, or on the highways connecting major cities, there are provisions for women at almost all mosques. Take, for instance, the Al Rajhi Mosque in Riyadh. Considered an architectural marvel, its Friday sermon is translated into seven languages. It accommodates 2,500 women in Friday prayers and hundreds in regular prayers. The special Taraweeh prayers in Ramadan are much favoured by the local women. The mosque even provides LCD screens for the hearing-impaired. The devotees can read on screen what the imam recites.

In the same city, one finds the Imam Turki Bin Abdullah Mosque, often favoured by the members of the royal family. A popular meeting point for scholars and learners, this mosque can take in around 17,000 people for prayer, the main hall is used by men and another hall is reserved for hundreds of women, who come here to establish prayer. For women, even better facilities are offered at the King Khalid Masjid in the heart of the city. Here, women have a floor to themselves and a separate, exclusive elevator to reach there. Not surprisingly, more women worshippers are of Arab origin and there is a low percentage of Indians and Pakistanis.

The scene is repeated across the country in Jeddah. The port city has the picturesque Hassan Anani Mosque in Jeddah Corniche. Built in 1985, it is a huge complex extending up to 2,400 metres. Often used by tourists and picnickers, the mosque has a large praying area for women. It is not unusual for families who come to enjoy their iftar at the Corniche to use the facilities at the mosque, which welcomes men and women with equal warmth.

The Hassan Anani Mosque is a symbol of a nation that has stayed honest to the Prophet's diktat when it comes to women's right to pray in the mosques. In fact, it could as well be the story of the entire West Asia region. From the more happening Jordan to Qatar, Kuwait, Bahrain, Oman and the UAE, women have mosques open to them throughout the day. Some even go in the wee hours for the optional Tahajjud prayers. In Dubai's upmarket Discovery Garden, there is Masjid Nakheel. The well-ventilated mosque attracts 1,500 worshippers on Fridays, every fourth person being a woman. There is ample space for women to pray, including a separate entrance, cloakroom and ablution space. In Bahrain, the Grand Al-Fateh Mosque has a floor dedicated to women. On Friday, around 400 to 500 women come to offer Jummah prayers.

'There is no concept of women being excluded from mosques in West Asia,' says Arshad Sheikh, press attaché of Jamaat-e-Islami Hind. He recalls,

In Step: A couple entering Bahrain's famous Grand mosque

> When I was in the Gulf, wherever I went all the mosques had a proper space for women. In Abu Dhabi, they always have a separate entrance for women. There is a common parking space, but from there itself, there is a division of path for men and women. The women have their own ablution centres, bathrooms. Even the mosques at petrol pumps have provisions for women.

These facilities, unfortunately, are not often used by the Indian women. The mosques see a higher percentage of the local UAE women and expatriate Arab women.

> If you see the population, the Asian expats are in a majority in the UAE. Of these, the Muslim expats are also substantial. But if you see in mosques, their footfall is not very high. Very few Indian or Pakistani women go to mosques regularly. They use the mosque

Mosques in Indonesia have clearly designated prayer space for women

> only in case of emergency, like if they are in a market and it is time for prayer, then they might go to the mosque, not otherwise.

This occasional use of the mosque by women comes to the fore at the beautiful Al-Noor Mosque at Sharjah Corniche. Though in regular prayers only a few women are seen, but on Ramadan the scene changes drastically. For Taraweeh, hundreds of women come to this mosque; at times the number even goes up to a thousand. Then there is Faisal Masjid in Sharjah, where women show up regularly for prayers. Then after the third prayer of the day, Asr, they stay back for some lessons on the Quran. Importantly, they manage the facility themselves without the intervention of any man, from the worshippers or the management committees.

The free and safe entry of women to the mosques is proved beyond doubt by the formidable Sultan Qaboos Grand Mosque in Oman's capital Muscat. The mosque complex, spread across 4,16,000 square metres, has the largest carpet and the largest chandelier. What it also has is a female prayer hall right at the entrance. It can accommodate up to 750 women in a prayer at one time. Outside the praying area, one can find women doing brisk business, selling dates and coffee. Nobody

Life and Beyond: Riyadh's famous Al Rajhi Mosque offers women not just a prayer hall but also facilities for the last rites. Here the female deceased can be bathed and are put in a shroud before the final prayers are offered. Scenes from the entrance to the women's prayer chambers and the cloakroom for the final ceremonial bath

objects either to their worship or their business. In fact, that is the beauty of the West Asian mosques—everybody minds his or her own business. If a man prays with a bare head, it does not get heads turning or another worshipper rushing to put a plastic cap on the head, as is often the case in the subcontinent. If a man prays with ankles covered, nobody gives a second look, again unlike the subcontinent where it invites glares. If a woman brings along an infant or her little children to the prayer space, nobody minds. If children run across the mosque premises, as is their wont, nobody objects. Worship though offered collectively is an individual act. To each his own. No attempt is made to impose the ideology of any Muslim body or sect on the worshipper.

This fact comes across most beautifully in the mosques in Turkey. Here, some people walk into a mosque, quickly offer their individual prayer without waiting for the *jamaat* or group prayer to begin and depart. Nobody minds, nobody asks questions. It is also the country where most mosques keep a little abaya or a cloak for women to cover themselves. It is a concession to local culture, where many women dress in Western attire, something which does not lend itself to prayer where worshippers are required to cover themselves from head to foot—men can pray with a bare head. Like the Indian mosques keep caps in reserve for a man who may not be carrying one, the mosques in Turkey keep cloaks and scarves ready on a hanger for a woman who might need one. It says a lot about the spirit of inclusion and openness prevalent at the mosques here. Turkey, like India, has a huge number of followers of the Hanafi sect. However, what is followed in India is not necessarily followed in Turkey. Cultural relativity rather than principles of a sect is paramount.

It all stems from the top. The President of Turkey, Recep Tayyip Erdogan, in October 2018, encouraged women and children of his country to go to the mosques. He urged the staff of Turkey's top religious body, Diyanet, the Directorate of Religious Affairs, to encourage women.

The *Hurriyet Daily News* reported Erdogan as saying that there was a 'taboo' against women praying in the mosques. 'There are mentalities that show this as Islam. But we need to get rid of these. These wrong taboos need to be destroyed now.'

Addressing the clerics, he said,

> It is my personal duty to encourage open discussion of all questions related to religion and mosques in this country. Is there a verse in the Quran or hadith that bars women from going to mosques? I have never heard of it or read of such a thing. My tutors have never taught me anything like that. These false beliefs must be dispelled.

Indeed.

And who is more unjust than those who prevent the name of Allah from being mentioned in His mosques and strive towards their destruction. It is not for them to enter them except in fear. For them in this world is disgrace, and they will have in the Hereafter a greater punishment.

—Surah Baqarah [verse 114],
The Glorious Quran

CHAPTER 13

Pakistan: A Slice of India

Noted writer Kamila Shamsie, who has never kept her fondness for Karachi a secret, once wrote about the sound at sunset in the city. Sound at sunset? Yes. She wrote about a vocal competition between its birds (mainly crows) and the muezzins, and went on to say that the actual competition in Karachi at sunset is between the muezzin of one mosque and that of the next; the birds don't stand a chance! What she did not go on to explore was the response to the muezzins' invitation—the azan is but an invitation for prayer, an invitation for success. Never mind. To that extent Karachi is like any Indian city. The muezzins at sunset could as well be competing at Triplicane in Chennai or Dharavi in Mumbai. Or even ITO in New Delhi. Not to forget good old Shahjahanabad in Bhopal or the vicinity of the famous Charminar in Hyderabad. And just to ensure that Karachi retains its Indian character of pre-Partition days, there are innumerable colonies named after Indian cities and townships. We have Madras Housing Cooperative Society, caught somewhat in a time warp considering Madras is now called Chennai in India. There is Lucknow Society too. Hard to ignore is the Aligarh Housing Society. Even smaller cities and towns, such as Meerut and Saharanpur, have societies named after them in Karachi, clearly showing that the men and women who migrated from India to Pakistan in 1947 took a little bit of the old nation to the emerging one. They went out of

India, but India remained etched in their minds. They took with them the age-old sociocultural practices too. Hence, in Karachi, even as muezzins compete to gain attention, very few women, like in India, accept the invitation. Fewer still venture out to establish prayer at a neighbouring mosque. Most are, like their sisters in India, unaware that they also should proceed to the nearest mosque at the time of prayer. For most, the call from the muezzin means a little break from watching television—the faithful usually switch to silence mode during azan. For pious women, it means rushing to perform ablution, then grabbing a prayer mat to offer their prayers. For men, it means heading to the mosque where most perform ablution and then offer prayer in a congregation. At the conclusion of prayer, they head home. It has been like that for generations in Karachi. Just like the way it is in Chennai, Kolkata or Lucknow.

Most mosques in the city are not women-friendly. Only a handful have more than one entry gate and hardly any mosque management committee thinks of women and the facilities they might need when the mosques are designed, or when they are renovated. That a woman may wish to come to the mosque for *itikaf*—a ten-day period spent in remembrance of Allah, away from the humdrum existence of everyday—or in Ramadan, this thought does not even cross the mind of the management committee. There are no women on the management committees of mosques, even if the foundation stone in some cases, as in Masjid-e-Ayesha in Karachi, is laid by a woman.

The scene is repeated elsewhere in Pakistan as well. Women do not figure in the scheme of things while building mosques in Lahore, Rawalpindi, Faisalabad or Khushab. Besides social ignorance about the rights of women, it leads to logistical problems too.

Take for instance, the all-new Masjid-e-Ayesha, built early in the new millennium in Karachi. Its gleaming marble floor tells you about its relatively recent origin. Its long *saffs* tell you that it attracts quite a few devotees. At any time, around forty men can stand in a row while establishing prayer. During daytime when most men are away at work,

Fight for Space: Women in Pakistan have managed to win space for themselves in newly constructed mosques in Islamabad. The story is different in age-old mosques

the mosque still attracts around 150 men, most retired and some working from home. On Fridays, the number goes up to a thousand. Incidentally, the mosque was initially named after Kaneez Fatima, the lady who laid its foundation stone. Later, it began to be called Masjid-e-Ayesha. Though named after the Prophet's wife, the mosque welcomes no women worshippers. From Fajr to Isha, all worshippers are men. Women are never seen at Masjid-e-Ayesha, an irony of sorts.

There is no provision for them. No separate entry or exit. No corridor to call their own. Not even a room, forget about a hall. It would appear from the lack of any publicised protest that women in the vicinity, the mosque is in a typical middle-class locality, do not deem the situation a blot on gender parity.

Most have probably never been to a mosque in the city. On a few occasions, when they go out to a mall or market to shop, they are content with finding a prayer room in the mall, which is reserved for them. The room is often not much more than a result of a kind gesture by a businessman who keeps a part of the showroom for prayer purpose, or even an entire shop. No such consideration seems to have dawned on the mosques or their management committees in the city. Unless, of course, one goes to a token mosque or two that are maintained by men owing allegiance to the Ahl-e-Hadith sect in Landhi Town or Saddar. In their mosques, women usually have a floor dedicated to them and turn out in good numbers for the Friday prayers. Incidentally, this is the sect that claims to be following the practices of the Prophet. Hence, the name. As far as accommodating women in the mosques is concerned, they are as good as their name.

A few brisk steps from Masjid-e-Ayesha, women gather for a spiritual discourse in Gulshan Kaneez Fatima. Almost every morning, after their husbands go to work, nearly thirty women gather at one of the neighbourhood houses to listen to a commentary of the Quran, understand the *tafsir* (commentary) of Maulana Maududi and maybe even listen to a talk on Ibn Kasir. They have been doing it for more than fifteen years now. Yet, it does not strike them that when Allah asks the faithful to establish prayer, He is addressing both men and women. Or that prayer can be offered in solitude, but can only be established in a *jamaat* or a group. It is like a brick supporting another brick to raise a wall and ultimately completing a building; a solitary brick by itself has limited use. It is the same for prayer. Embedded deep into their psyche is the Hadith related to Umm Umayd, who was told to pray at home. Forgotten is the Prophet's more general Hadith of the best prayer for a man being in the first row and that for a woman in the last row. Clearly, indoctrination of centuries won't be washed away so easily. Not surprisingly, they do not even consult any of the modern commentaries of the Quran, confining themselves to the age-old books.

Karachi, though, is not the only Pakistani city with a huge preponderance of men-only mosques. Go up north to Lahore, Rawalpindi, Multan or Faisalabad, and the story stays the same. It is just a bit of Sindhi or Urdu sandpapered away, a bit of Punjabi added. The exclusion of women stays in place. In relatively less frenetic towns, such as Khushab too, the male dominance comes through the presence of only men in these mosques. Considering that most mosques here are in the residential areas, with some indistinguishable from common houses from a distance, it defies explanation for how the mosques here register no footfall of women. Interestingly, the place is well used by Jamaat-e-Islami activists; the body has its district office here too. The Tanzeem-e-Islami supporters also are in good number here. All this fails to change the demographic profile of the mosques in this region.

Most old mosques are built in the traditional Indo-Persian manner with glazed glass and tiles complementing a bigger central dome painted in white or green, for instance, the Dada Gora Masjid and the Chappar Sharif. The new mosques lack personality: the same set of red rugs, similar air-conditioners, Italian tiles and a marble floor.

New or old, the mosques are an all-male domain. It is forgotten by men and women alike that when the Prophet was approached by some women for exemption from attendance at the Fajr prayers, he did not grant it. This is when the roads were neither metalled nor safe, and women had to travel long distances in the wee hours to make it to the Prophet's mosque in time for the Fajr prayer. In Khushab, many, if they so prefer, would not have to walk for more than a few minutes. This few minutes' walk to the masjid is taking more than a lifetime.

Again, much like in India, women continue to have their way at the tombs of the city, be it Sakhi Shah Maroof Khushab or

Darbar-e-Badshah. It is only when they have to pray at a mosque that Islamic tradition and talk of gender parity are cast aside.

Interestingly, things get remarkably different and better for women, as one travels up north to Islamabad. The capital is dotted with modern mosques, such as the Jama Masjid in Defence Housing Authority area. Here, as indeed at many other recent mosques, the doors are open to women. The Jama Masjid not only offers a special prayer section to women replete with green carpets, white marble wudu khana and a lattice entry gate, it also offers a clear pathway to women. Right from parking, the passage gets delineated. Though inside the prayer hall women's attendance continues to be thin. While the mosque takes in about a thousand men on Fridays, women are less than a hundred. The scene is repeated at other mosques, where women enter from the northern gate and men from the south. On the motorway also women are provided prayer facilities adjacent to the men's section.

All this is a recent addition possible partly due to the work-related travel the Pakistani men have had to undertake. Men who work in the Gulf either send in money as an act of charity to mosques or come back home after a long stint abroad. Besides money they come back with their vistas widened and greater exposure to inclusive mosques in the Gulf and elsewhere. Suddenly, it seems no longer a big deal for the mosques to welcome women! Interestingly, the devout at the mosque have extreme profiles. While most people in the mosques, such as the Faisal Masjid or Jama Masjid, come from the upper strata of the society, men who can dip into their pocket to give a donation of a few thousand rupees to the mosque, there are others who only survive by earning just a few rupees a day. The longest trip they would have undertaken in their life would be from their village to Islamabad in search of livelihood. In the absence of exposure to rest of the world, they always leave their women at home, even on Fridays, when they come to the mosque. The better travelled men bring their spouses along. Some bring them along on Fridays and others for Taraweeh during Ramadan. Many more bring their spouses on Eid. This gives the nation hope that one day the historical anomaly can be corrected. And women can be conspicuous, if not equal, partners in the planning and running of the mosques.

However, lessons learnt at the Prophet's Mosque and Corniche mosques will have to wait another day for implementation. Today, it is the sentiment that surrounds Masjid-e-Ayesha that dominates the discourse in religious circles. In the old city of Lahore and elsewhere, women can contribute to building mosques, but cannot pray there. Little boys continue to hold the hand of their fathers as they walk down to the mosque. Old men hold on to the hands of their young sons as they find their way to the sacred space. The girls stay at home with their mothers and grandmothers. There is a prayer mat. There is the inner room. The more things change, the more they stay the same.

You have an excellent model in the Messenger of Allah, for all who put their hope in Allah and the Last Day and remember Allah much.

—Surah al-Ahzab [verse 21]

CHAPTER 14

Exceptions to the Practice

Ahl-e-Hadith Mosques: As the Prophet Advised

In the hustle bustle of traffic and not far from the blaring horns of ambulances stands the Rahmani Masjid in south-east Delhi. Not particularly remarkable in its architecture, the mosque is among a handful in the city to open its premises to women. Its basement, with a capacity of around 400 people, is reserved for women. They have a separate entrance, wudu khana and exit. They can, in fact, hope to arrive and exit untouched by the male gaze. The hall gets packed only on Fridays and the special *salah* on Eid when women often come in with their little children. On the remaining days, there is only a trickle of worshippers. In the neighbourhood, the mosque is known as Ahl-e-Hadith Masjid or Ahl-e-Hadith hazarat ki masjid. Nobody bothers to call the mosque by its name. Just the sect that maintains the mosque is the identifiable point.

This is not peculiar to this mosque. It is almost a norm with the mosques maintained or favoured by the Ahl-e-Hadith followers, who bring up roughly 3 per cent of Muslims in the country, the community claims to follow the practices of Prophet Muhammad in letter and spirit. Though not many questions are asked of their practices, every time somebody does raise a fuss about the constant presence of women in their mosques, the answer is provided calmly by taking recourse, predictably, to the Hadith and sunnah of the Prophet. One is reminded of what the Prophet once advised his followers to do after he would be gone: 'hold on to the Quran and Sunnah, the practice of the Prophet.' Needless to reiterate neither the Quran prohibits women from establishing prayers at a mosque nor did the Prophet ever ask women to keep away from the mosques. In fact, as modern-day men are reminded by Ahl-e-Hadith brothers, the Prophet asked men not to prevent women from going to the mosque.

The Prophet laid a lot of stress on simplicity and reminded the faithful to keep their mosques simple without any ostentation. He wanted the faithful to be able to connect with the Almighty in their prayer rather than be overawed by the majesty of the mosque. His advice is well taken at many Ahl-e-Hadith mosques. There is respectful inclusion of women and there is hardly any ostentation, often no big chandeliers inside. At times, the mosques have no domes to distinguish them from other structures in the vicinity. Also, the prayer call is brief and people are given time to assemble for the prayer rather than having to rush to the mosque immediately after hearing the azan. This is particularly true at the time of Maghrib (sunset) prayers where, invariably, a few minutes are allowed to lapse after the muezzin pronounces the azan. This helps men and women in the vicinity to perform ablution after hearing the call, and then head to the mosque. This is in stark contrast to most other mosques in the country, where Maghrib azan is followed only seconds later by the formal prayer.

For proof, one can visit Phatak Punjabian in Shahjahanabad or Old Delhi and find the locals referring to a mosque of broken tile pieces as Ahl-e-Hadith Masjid. The mosque is bereft of architectural beauty yet it is appealing because of its simplicity. In comparison to the more happening Lal Masjid barely a few yards away, this is almost a sober and calm mosque, where the emphasis is on women's privacy. The mosque is a closed structure giving no chance to any passerby to take a quick look at the devotees inside.

Not just in Delhi but Ahl-e-Hadith mosques keep women in the reckoning at the planning stage in almost all cities and towns. All the needs of women worshippers are respected. Their section, like the men's section, has religious books, small tables for keeping them and chairs for those who cannot stand in prayer. Occasionally, not often, hijab or a dupatta is available for those who may not be dressed as per the requirements of prayer. Almost every big city in India has at least a couple of Ahl-e-Hadith mosques. For instance, in Chennai most of the women-friendly mosques belong to Ahl-e-Hadith, such as the Anjuman Himayath-e-Islam that offers facilities for five daily prayers. It attracts around 500 women on Fridays. In Kerala, besides hundreds of Jamaat-e-Islami Hind mosques, there are dozens of Salafi and Ahl-e-Hadith mosques welcoming women visitors. The scene is the same in Mumbai, Hyderabad, Bhopal, Lucknow and Jaipur. Here women come in not just at the time of congregational prayer, but even later to catch up with their individual prayers. In Ramadan, many office-going women hop over during a break from work to read the Quran.

So, what makes these mosques attractive? Their inclusiveness and their focus on abiding by the advice of the Prophet: hold on to the Quran and the Sunnah. Without screaming their lungs out, the sect stays respectfully different from the Hanafis who bring up a vast majority of followers in the subcontinent. In welcoming women into the mosques, they silence those critics who take recourse to Caliph Umar's alleged prohibition of women. Again, no din is created and the opponents are merely reminded that the Quran's teachings are forever. Noted Ahl-e-Hadith scholar Maulana Mukhtar Ahmad Nadvi in an Urdu book *Kya Musalman Khwatin Ka Masjid Mein Aana Fitna Hai* (Is the Entry of Women into Mosques a Source of Strife) argued,

> that if allowing women to colleges, to work in offices and factories, voting in elections, going to the market or using public transport,

> all of which entail mixing with men, are not considered sources of fitna (strife or mischief), how could praying in a mosque, God's house, be considered a dangerous threat?

Nadvi and other Ahl-e-Hadith scholars draw their inspiration from the early Islamic period, to the times of the Prophet himself, when women too participated enthusiastically in congregational prayers in the mosque. They also remind us of the Hadith narrated by Ayesha, the wife of the Prophet, where she is reported to have said that women used to attend even the Fajr (dawn) prayers by *jamaat*.

Nadvi in his book cited another Hadith narrated by Anas, a companion of the Prophet, and mentioned in the collections of Bukhari and Sahih Muslim, to suggest that women used to worship in the mosques along with their children. Of course, the Ahl-e-Hadith community members remind those opposing women's entry into the mosques of another Hadith related by Abu Hurairah, a companion of the Prophet. According to this Hadith, which too finds space in Bukhari and Sahih Muslim, regarded as authentic Hadith books by most believers, women during the time of the Prophet and the caliphs even had the right to admonish the imam by clapping their hands if he made any mistake in reciting the prayer.

The Ahl-e-Hadith scholars point out that it is the fundamental right of a woman to pray at a mosque, and it is the duty of those running the mosque to provide them with the facilities needed for a prayer. Keeping them away from the mosques is tantamount to keeping half the society away from guidance. To deny them this right, Nadvi asserted in his book, 'is to openly defy the Quranic verse that speaks of those who debar people from worshipping in the mosque as oppressors (zalim). The Quran warns such people that they would be the victims of divine wrath in the hereafter.' Also, the Ahl-e-Hadith mosques receive more women worshippers on Fridays as the women of the community try to live up to the instruction given in Surah Jumuah, wherein the faithful are told to leave everything when it is time for Jumuah prayers. 'O you who believe! When the call is recited for prayer on Friday (the day of assembly) hurry sincerely to the Remembrance of Allah, and leave behind the business (and traffic): That is best for you if you only knew,' says the Quran. The members of the Ahl-e-Hadith community seem to know.

Enter into Islam entirely.

—Surah Baqarah [verse 208],
The Glorious Quran

CHAPTER 15
The Winds of Change

Quietly, almost imperceptibly, a silent movement for women's right to pray in the mosque is gaining traction. More and more mosques and maulanas are realising that in the days, months and years to come, the movement could capture the attention of the wider society. Some are also realising the injustice done to women in the name of their security, or selective usage of scriptures. They are beginning to take remedial action. Maybe reluctantly, maybe half-heartedly, maybe to atone for the wrongs of the past, but more and more mosques are being opened to members of both genders. The change is perceptible to the discerning.

Take for instance, a little known Gulhar Wali Masjid in Old Delhi, the Madina Masjid in Aurangabad, another mosque in Parli in Maharashtra or Masjid Bhoori Bhatyari, located in the heart of India's capital, opposite India's Fleet Street. All these mosques have opened at least a part of the building to women to come and offer their prayers. In the past, women were either not allowed or if a woman did come in, she could at best, hope to offer her prayer in a secluded corner. Not anymore, as these and many other mosques have reserved rooms for women. Not often are women given facilities of ablution or a separate entry yet, but at least, now they can hope to offer prayers standing alongside their sisters. The rooms in all these cases are small, in fact, almost tiny. But even in their smallness they signify a giant leap for the community, which has often pretended that men are supposed to come to the mosques and women are supposed to pray at home only. This more-than-a-century old dichotomy is beginning to break. It is very early days, but the winds of change are blowing in the world of the faithful of the subcontinent. A little example of the march of progressive forces comes from a small segment of the improvised prayer hall at the Maulana Azad National Urdu University in Hyderabad. The university has no mosque, but on Fridays men gather in a hall that is usually used for indoor sports. They offer their Jumuah prayers there, and disperse, leaving the facility to sportsmen. Now, however, the girl students have asserted themselves, and won for themselves a little space, covered with cloth curtains to the left of the hall. Every Friday, a handful of girls gather here and pray behind the same imam at the same time.

Then in Ramadan, in the summer of 2019, heart-warming news trickled in from the Kashmir valley. In the strife-torn state, the Muttahida Majlis-e-Ulema (MMU), an organization including various religious bodies, decided to dedicate the Ramadan sermons to women and issues affecting them. Mirwaiz Umar Farooq, the MMU patron, told the media, 'We will focus on domestic violence, dowry, education. We will also talk about the need to open mosques for women.' He added, 'We have our old mosques where we have a separate space for women. But the new mosques that we have built don't have such provisions. That is a serious issue.'

Again, this is a small step that could turn into a giant leap in the years to come.

Shahi Jama Masjid, Old Delhi

All roads to the historic Jama Masjid were closed due to vehicular traffic. Thousands walked down from Daryaganj, Chandni Chowk, Ajmeri Gate and Sui Walan to the 17th century mosque. As Isha, the concluding prayer of the day, was about to commence, there was not an inch of space available in the mosque, which can accommodate up to 25,000 worshippers. Men had positioned themselves for prayer

Inside by Right: Women have had their own space in the historic Jama Masjid of Old Delhi. They pray as part of the congregation

on each of its thirty-nine stairs. There were intrepid young men on the tips of their toes at the Shahi Darwaza, watching a sea of people moving towards the mosque. None of them could make it to the mosque. Realising the futility of the effort, many had spread their prayer mat on the road itself. First one man, then another, then yet another. The road from the mosque to Matia Mahal could as well have been a corridor of Jama Masjid.

Even as the imam stood up to begin the prayer, hundreds of men jostled with each other to perform wudu. In the *dalan*, there were hundred-odd women. Some had brought their prayer mats along and others had hurriedly gone through the motions in the presence of uncountable men. Clearly, it was a rare Isha prayer in congregation for them. Today, 8 July 2009, was not a usual day. The 12th Shahi Imam of Jama Masjid, Syed Abdullah Bukhari, had passed away. He had breathed his last at the All India Institute of Medical Sciences around 9.30 in the morning. Post the Isha prayer he was to be buried. Along with thousands of men, the women too wanted to have one final look at the imam they held dear. Most were not able to catch a glimpse, the byre being too far from their view. Yet, on that day, many had left behind their aged parents and small children to come to the masjid to offer Isha, and then maybe attend the funeral prayer as well before going back home. Among them were women in their 40s and 50s who had seen the imam stand up for the community at the time of the Emergency. They were young girls then, but the imam's robust stature, his zest and energy were hard to ignore even for a child. Almost every Friday, the imam issued a new warning to the Government, speaking out against relocation of shops around the masjid, or shielding men and women during the sterilisation drive of Congress leader Sanjay Gandhi. Not much before the Emergency, he had been arrested following the communal riots in February 1974, only to come out soon after as the masses protested. His word carried weight. Post Emergency, he had become something of a cult figure for Muslims, with news trickling in that he had been offered the post of Vice President in 1977. It never materialised, but thanks to the imam's fearless ways, the attendance at Jama Masjid improved by leaps and bounds. Not just men, even women started coming to the mosque in larger numbers. A veranda to the left of the water pond, and close to the gate, was reserved for them. On bad days, it was half full. On good days, it was overflowing with women. There were a few Eid prayers post-1975, when there were so many women that the veranda could not accommodate them all. Some tried to step down on the platform where men stood. They were hurriedly told to move upstairs. So, on the roof of the masjid, the women prayed. It was a sight to behold! Thousands of men with the estimates reaching up to 40,000 in and around the mosque and hundreds of women in the corridor and many more on the roof.

Imam Abdullah Bukhari left this world in 2009, but the gumption women derived from his actions continues to drive them even today. More women come to Shah Jahan's Jama Masjid than anywhere in the city. Many contend there are more women worshippers here than in the most mosques in Kerala or even Ahmedabad, where Jaali Wali Masjid is frequented regularly by women. Bukhari, in many ways, helped break the stereotype of a mosque in the country. He concentrated not on academic debates or those dealing with the interpretation of the meaning of the Quran, but sought to blend religion and politics like never before. It also meant he kept some time separate for women worshippers who could come to him with their issues for guidance. It led to a separate wudu khana for women. At some point, in the summer of 1996, the women's section came to have its own curtains, meant not so much to guard them from any possible prying eyes, but to protect them from the harsh *loo*, the hot wind that blows in this part of the world from May to July. This was also the year some clerics around the mosque started a campaign against women going to Jama Masjid.

In smaller mosques around the historic Jama Masjid, the clerics would gather in the *hujra* (room) of an imam, talking in whispers about the need to stop women from going to mosques. 'Picnic bana liya hai' (They have made it a picnic), the clerics complained and sought a fatwa against their entry to the masjid. Some were imams of such small mosques that they could not take in more than fifty worshippers; others led a relatively larger congregation, but leading a congregation of 200 men is one thing and taking on a man who often led 25,000 is quite another. No cleric mustered up the courage to speak to Bukhari directly, preferring to use local Urdu newspapers besides hangers-on around Bukhari to get their message through. Whatever it was, the message failed to move Bukhari. Also, the fatwa never came; the actual scholars of the Quran knew the scriptures do not forbid women from going to a mosque. What did come was an assurance from Bukhari: 'Women were welcome in the masjid. All women, not just Muslim women. The only condition being they should be fully covered.'

The support of the imam had a ripple effect, with women starting to go for the Jumuah prayers to mosques in places, such as Lucknow, Patna and Bhopal. In Old Delhi itself, women, who used to attend night schools after putting their children to bed, were among the keenest worshippers. At night they went to a school in Lal Kuan or Turkman Gate to learn the alphabet. During daytime, they came at least once to Jama Masjid to join their sisters who had been doing it for much longer. *The Statesman* reported,

> Mosques are no longer a monopoly of men, as women in Kerala, Bangalore, Lucknow and now Delhi have proved. Sample this: A religious congregation is assembling at Noida. A score-odd men of all ages have gathered at the time of Isha prayers. There is nothing unusual about the assembly. That is until a middle-aged man objects to the presence of three women amidst them. 'Let men attain enlightenment first, then they can educate the women. After all, they have not been coming to mosques for the last 1,400 years,' is the refrain of a not-so-enlightened soul .... 'Women can pray in the privacy of their home. Yeh sab feminism ki den hai.' (All this—act of women coming out to pray—is a gift of feminism.) Not one to be browbeaten, (Rehana) Khan comes up with a clincher: 'Women have merely been exempted. They have not been debarred from praying in mosques.'[1]

The article concluded on a positive note. 'It may be a trickle at the moment but soon it is going to be a stream,' the report said. The stream is yet to materialise. But thanks to Jama Masjid, appropriately built on a lofty plinth, women have something to look forward to. The mosque gave them shelter at the time of Partition. It accommodated many during the excesses of the Emergency. Little wonder, women braved all odds to be at the

[1] *The Statesman*, 1997. Section II, Delhi; Mosques No Longer Monopoly of Men-Only. 19 September 1997.

masjid when Bukhari bade goodbye to the world in 2009. Today, it holds out hope to all, including members of the third gender who stand for prayer every Friday in the men's section. They seldom find receptive worshippers elsewhere. The Shahi Jama Masjid embraces them all: men, women and transgenders, all on the same platform and the same floor.

Jama Masjid, New Delhi

The summer of 2014 came with myriad challenges. Even as rest of the country was engrossed in the general elections that brought with them hopes of better days, the worshippers at Jama Masjid, New Delhi, wrestled with problems uniquely their own. For years, the worshippers had gathered in good numbers at the early 20th-century red sandstone mosque built to cater to the needs of Lutyens' Delhi after the Imperial Capital was shifted to Delhi from Calcutta in 1911. Located amidst a wide expanse of Government of India offices, its central location almost opposite the Parliament House spoke as much about the secular fabric of the nation as the fact that a prayer house disturbed none. Not even politicians endlessly riven along party lines. For government servants, the long line of clerks and officers, the bureaucrats and diplomats, even some ministers and Members of Parliament (MPs) when the House was in session, the Jama Masjid (New Delhi) provided a comfortable avenue for a peaceful prayer. Its maroon carpets, brown-tiled walls and the newly installed air-conditioners meant nobody was out of his or her comfort zone in the communion with the Almighty.

In the spring of 2014 though, a part of the ceiling of the first floor prayer hall collapsed. Plaster peeled off. Soon fears were expressed about the safety and durability of the mosque itself, with the imam Muhibullah Nadwi not ready to take a chance with the safety of the devotees. The mosque was set for an overhaul, its ceiling needed to be redone, its walls to be plastered afresh, its wudu khana to be rebuilt too. As the work that started in late spring continued into peak summer, the worshippers knew not a day of ease. Every afternoon, as they came from their offices for Zuhr salat, prayer itself became a challenge. With the mosque now occupied by rubble, bricks, tiles and other raw materials for construction, men had to pray outside in the open verandah, where all that shielded them from the relentless heat of Delhi's summer was the occasional shadow of the mosque. Sometimes, they offered their prayers near the late President Fakhruddin Ali Ahmed's tomb, and others near the threshold of the mosque where listening to the imam became a challenge amidst blaring horns of vehicles passing by on the Red Cross Road. As men stood shoulder to shoulder, fasting in the month of Ramadan, beads of sweat formed over their foreheads and trickled all the way down to their face and beyond. Some mumbled, a few grumbled. Yet, most took it in their stride. The short-term inconvenience was like the toll tax they paid for a better mosque in the not-so-distant future.

And what a mosque the New Delhi Jama Masjid turned out to be, by fall 2014: marble flooring and stairway, exquisite inlay work on the ceiling, intricate woodwork, an expansive ablution centre, new toilets, expensive chandeliers and a few verses of the Quran painted by a calligrapher on the front wall! With tower air-conditioners standing tall against every alternate niche and green Persian carpets bringing up the prayer hall, the mosque became a tourist spot of sorts. In Ramadan of 2015, every weekend tourists descended to admire its beauty and grandeur. On the tourist map, it became an irresistible showpiece. In the evening, post-Isha, the last prayer of the day, men of Old Delhi hopped over to see a mosque that rivalled the best in West Asia in its elegance. Some even brought with them the women of the family. For most of the wives, mothers, sisters, daughters, it was a rare outing to a mosque. Many had never seen a mosque from the inside. In fact, after one late evening visit, many of them came back a day or two later; this time for Maghrib, the evening prayer that also marks the breaking of the fast.

And in that little action was a breath of fresh air. The mosque offered complimentary iftar to all the fasting people. It included a small tray of chicken biryani, fresh fruit salad, packaged juice, a couple of dates and some fritters. Every evening nearly 200 men gathered for the iftar, sitting cross-legged in the corridor used for prayer only on special occasions. Importantly, every evening, some two dozen women gathered for the iftar in a room earmarked for them. The food items remained the same, the servers also remained the same. They, however, made sure that the food was ready before the women were! Thus, a working woman who came in only a few minutes before the iftar time was often pleased to see her food tray ready and waiting for her. It was a pleasant but rare experience for most women. Beyond Shah Jahan's Jama Masjid in Old Delhi, it was unthinkable for women to step into a mosque for iftar. In a city with hundreds of mosques dotting the landscape, particularly in the areas with a predominance of Muslim population, there was no other mosque that offered a room to call their own and iftar to have with sisters in faith. The women responded positively to the gesture of the New Delhi Jama Masjid's imam, particularly those who worked in offices in the vicinity. Iftar over, almost all women stayed in to offer Maghrib prayer by *jamaat*. With their inhibitions about visiting a mosque gone, many of them came back on the following Fridays to offer the Jumuah prayers alongside their sisters. Like the men in the main hall, women also stood shoulder to shoulder with fellow women in their own section. What's more, the room not only gave them complete privacy, but also an opportunity to recite the Quran, read its commentary and even rest for a while. Just the way a mosque should.

The room became a reality thanks to the vision of ace business magnate Yusuf Ali from Kerala, who financed the mosque's uplift programme. With his vast exposure to West Asia due to his sizable business interests, Ali understood that a mosque was not for men alone. Hence, he happily financed the facility for women worshippers here. Most regular worshippers were happy too; a lot of them were office-goers who worked in various government departments in the vicinity. Some, however, protested. And protested vehemently, they opposed the idea of women entering the masjid. They sought political intervention besides knocking on the doors of the All India Wakf Board. To no avail though, as most people in a position of authority realised there was nothing un-Islamic about keeping a room solely for women devotees.

The discontent seems to have settled down now. And the mosque continues to be favoured by women, not just for the Friday prayers, or special occasions like Ramadan or Eid, but also to offer their own private prayers as and when they get a break from work. Just as men do.

What is more, the mosque seems to have inspired others in the vicinity. Similar facilities are on the anvil at the Pandara Road and India Gate mosques, while at the age-old Masjid Bhoori Bhatyari on Bahadur Shah Zafar Marg a beginning has been made with the reservation of a small room at the entrance for women. Even though it is a small section, women still have a dedicated passage to it with elementary facilities.

Not many would say it in as many words, but the beginning made in 2014 is causing a ripple effect.

Jamaat-e-Islami Hind, Markaz

Maulana Abul Ala Maududi, the founder of Jamaat-e-Islami, was known to be the most conservative of all Muslim leaders. Many accused him of being too orthodox and too regimented in his thinking. Maududi though in his own understated ways, understood the pulse of the Muslim community. Not only did he strive to give an ideological grooming to the next generation, he also tried to inculcate in the members of the Jamaat the values of an Islamic way of life. Though common people often found his commentary of the Quran too arduous to read or too straitjacketed in approach, it was this understanding of faith that enabled Jamaat-e-Islami Hind to open its portals to women.

Much before Tablighi Jamaat, the largest Muslim body founded almost a hundred years ago by Maulana Ilyas set up its women's wing, the Jamaat-e-Islami felt the pulse of the times and opened not just its mosques to women, but also gave them membership of the electoral body. Today, women make up 19 per cent of the Jamaat's members and 29 per cent of its workers. The Jamaat has a woman among its secretaries. Besides, in the representative body of 150 people that chooses the amir (president) of the Jamaat, there are 22 women.[2]

Inevitably, the Jamaat has opened the prayer sections of its mosques across the country. While the main mosque, the Markaz, is in Delhi, there are some 400 mosques in Kerala under the maintenance of the Jamaat. All remain open to women visitors.

It did not start off without proper planning. Realising that there are numerous Hadiths that give women the right to go to mosques and that the Quran does not prohibit women from entering places of worship, the Jamaat, in the early 1990s, decided to reserve a section of its mosque at its headquarters in Okhla, south-east Delhi. A little before that, the Jamaat opened its Markaz to women, to come, discuss and debate. Soon, at the Jamaat's mosque at the centre, a women's wing was created, where women could come to pray as and when they wanted. While during the daily prayers, there were only a handful of women who availed of the facility, over a period time, the word spread that Markaz had a provision for women to pray by *jamaat*. Gradually, more women started coming to the mosque. Today, roughly 200 women turn up almost every Friday for establishing prayer. It does not compare favourably with almost a thousand men, who offer Friday prayers here, but it is a beginning, and the Jamaat is faced with centuries

[2] Based on my interactions with the Jamaat officials at the Jamaat Headquarters in Delhi.

of indoctrination of Muslim women in the subcontinent due to which it does not even come to the minds of most women that they can go to the mosque for prayers. Deep down in their psyche the women grow up with notions of men going to masjid and women going to an inner room at home for salat.

But things are changing, albeit slowly. While on Fridays, and indeed other days, men have a large portion of the hall reserved for them at the Markaz Masjid and women have the left wing, where they can hear the imam clearly and at the same time stay away from the gaze of men. On occasions like Eid, women come out in larger numbers and are entitled to a much bigger space on the lawns of the Markaz as well. On Eid, many more women come for salat. Accordingly, the women's section, to the left of the main prayer hall, is completely occupied. Before this concrete hall, a pink cloth partition used to announce the section from the laws of the complex. Interestingly, women who come here are often accompanied by their husbands or fathers. It is obvious they enjoy the support of the men in the family, who do not think it is un-Islamic for a woman to go to a mosque to pray.

They are, however, the lucky ones. Most Muslim women, on Eid, do not get a chance to offer the special salat. With most mosques being virtually out of bounds, and most men believing that on Eid men go out for prayer while women cook and clean at home, there is limited scope for women to step out and establish festive prayer. The Jamaat-e-Islami's women's section is understandably patronised by women from far and near. While many women come from the neighbourhood, most drive down from far-off colonies. While this says a lot about their zest for offering salat in a congregation, it speaks ill of most mosques in the residential areas.

This change, limited as it is, has not been easy. A vast majority of Muslim bodies, and Muslim men, still nurse the notion that mosques are for men only. The Jamaat too was confronted with similar opposition in the early days. People from the Hanafi sect—according to an estimate, 80 per cent of Indian Muslims are from the Hanafi sect—opposed the move. However, they had to beat a retreat when confronted with a cold fact: men and women perform tawaf together in hajj and umrah, how can women be excluded from a masjid anywhere? Indeed. Women are exempted from attending daily prayers at the mosques, not prohibited. The decision to go or not go has to be that of the woman concerned.

Whoever builds a mosque only for the sake of winning Allah`s pleasure, Allah will build for him a house in Paradise.

—Prophet Muhammad

CHAPTER 16

India in the Past: Medieval Mosques Built by Women

Almost 800 years to this day, Delhi Sultanate ruler Razia Sultan carved out a piece of history. In fact, two. The first was, obviously, being elevated to the throne in the early 13th century and becoming thereby the first woman to rule over Delhi. The favoured daughter of Iltutmish, Razia rose to the throne ahead of half-brother Muiz ud-din Bahram. At that time also the ulema initially opposed her candidature. She was sincere, wise, adept at administration and capable of leading the Sultanate in a war. The only handicap she faced, according to them, was her gender. However, as she enjoyed the confidence of her father Iltutmish, she defied the odds to claim the throne. The other feat was notched up with her ascension itself. In the run up to assuming control of the Sultanate, she went to Quwwatul Islam Masjid in Mehrauli, said to be the first mosque of North India. She did so on a Friday when the mosque would have maximum worshippers; and sought the support of the devout for her claim to the throne. Importantly, she did not call herself Sultana, the feminine of Sultan. She referred to herself as the Sultan. With her address at the Quwwatul Islam Masjid, Razia not only blazed a trail for other women to go to masjid but also to build masjids. The khutbah too was read in her name, the first time ever in India's recorded history. She used to travel without a veil and used to ride horses and elephants. It is

Women Omitted: The famous Tajul Masjid in Bhopal was built by the begums of Bhopal, but there is no space for women inside the mosque

believed that she used to go to mosques and madrasas. Her patronage of khanqahs and madrasas is well known, especially the one that was associated with Minhaj Siraj Juzjani, the author of Tabaqat-e-Nasiri. He was considered a Sheikh-ul Islam under Razia Sultan.

Muslim women had things pretty good in medieval times. Politically, they were taken into confidence by the emperors who consulted them at every stage. The stories of Noor Jahan, who wielded great control over the Mughal king Jahangir, are also well known to need reiteration. The founder of the Mughal dynasty Zahiruddin Babur too is said to have consulted his women, his mother, his wives and daughters, before venturing out for a battle. In Delhi, we have the 16th century Khairul Manazil Masjid built by Maham Anga, the foster mother of the greatest Mughal ruler Jalaluddin Akbar. The Khairul Manazil Masjid, built in 1561 by Anga, is said to be the first mosque in Delhi to be commissioned by a woman, the same woman who was virtually the ruler of the empire in the early years of Akbar, as the Mughal scion was too young to fulfil the responsibilities of an emperor. Though there is little historical evidence to prove if Anga herself came to attend the prayer sessions here, what is proven beyond doubt is that she was instrumental in the construction of the mosque. Incidentally, many Mughal princesses after her undertook the construction of mosques as an act of piety without necessarily visiting the mosques for daily prayers. In the case of Khairul Manazil, Anga hired the services of her trusted relative Shahabuddin Ahmad Khan, who was also a minister of the empire. The mosque's central arch has an inscription that clearly reveals that the mosque was built by Maham Anga. The mosque had a madrasa attached to it, probably funded by Anga herself for Islamic education of children.

At around the same time, and also during the age of Jahangir and Shah Jahan, we have Mughal miniatures showing them riding horses and moving around without a veil. Often they dictated their *nikahnama*s and incorporated conditions like monogamy, no instant triple talaq, or investing in themselves the right to divorce through Talaq-e-tafweez. They continued to build mosques, madrasas and *sarai*s. According to some historians, they also graced the mosques, at least on special occasions like Eid, or when a new emperor took the reins of the empire, and had the khutbah read under his name as a sign of legitimacy.

Though there is little documentary evidence, it is fair to believe they offered prayers in the mosques if one looks at the architecture of the Sultanate and the Mughal period closely. For instance, there is a Tughlaq era mosque in Wazirabad in Delhi. The mosque has an elevated chamber shielded by lattice walls. There are some historians who believe it was meant for the kings. However, as the kings usually entered from the main gate, called the Shahi Darwaza, it is fair to believe it was meant for the royal women who entered and departed from such a gate after offering their prayers at the mosque. Most historians believe that in the Wazirabad Masjid, the place behind the lattice walls was reserved for women worshippers. Men prayed in the main hall and women in their own specified section, behind the lattice walls.

Similarly, if you go to Bengal, there in Hazrat-e-Pandua we have Adina Masjid, one of the largest mosques in India. Hailing from the 15th century, it is a much bigger mosque than Quwwatul Islam Masjid. The prayer chamber here is elevated with a lattice wall and a raised mihrab, a semi-circular niche. Many mosques in medieval India can be said to have been graced by royal women, and even those from the families of nobles. There is no a single piece of historical evidence to show that women were prohibited from going to the mosques, and there is no record of ulema issuing a fatwa against the entry of women into mosques.

Not just mosques, women went to Sufi khanqahs and dargahs too, and are said to have participated with great zest in singing Sufiana Kalam. From the early 13th century when Qutubuddin Aibak laid the foundation of the Mamluk dynasty to the time of the latter Mughals in the 18th and 19th centuries, women were consistent in their patronage of khanqahs. As most dargahs and khanqahs had mosques attached to them, it is fair to conclude that women would enter them as the Sufis did not express any rigidity. For instance, Nizamuddin Auliya held out for musical gatherings or *samaa*, and was able to convince the Sultanate rulers too of the same, despite stiff opposition from the Hanafi scholars of the age who believed music to be haram (prohibited) in Islam. Inside the mosques, we find no clear markers prohibiting the entry of women beyond a certain stage.

It all began to change with the decline of the Mughals and the coming of the British. As conservatism was the order of the day, women began to be excluded from both mosques and cemeteries. They were not allowed to enter the mosques for spiritual elevation. They were denied the right to offer prayers at the grave of their near and dears ones in the cemetery. All along, women continued to go for hajj. In medieval as also modern times, women were never denied the right to go on hajj where, like men and women from other countries, they established prayers in both Makkah and Medina, where they went to the last resting place of the wives of the Prophet as also his companions. Yet, when they came back home, a different kind of Islam ruled their lives. Call it the impact of the local culture, but this Indianised form of Islam meant women could build mosques or take part in financing them, but could not offer regular prayers inside them. Today, women cannot go for prayers to the mosques that their fellow women built hundreds of years ago. The most conspicuous case being of the famous Fatehpuri Masjid in Old Delhi, where the local residents cannot recall any occasion when women gathered to offer prayer in a group, or the Taj-ul-Masajid in Bhopal. It is the largest mosque in India, but it has not been able to spare a room or hall for women. The biases are more pronounced today than at any time in the Islamic history in India.

Akbarabadi Masjid

A little under two decades ago when construction started for Delhi Metro Rail Corporation's link to Old Delhi, most residents of Old Delhi heard of Akbarabadi Masjid for the first time. As news poured in of plans to dig up the Netaji Subhash Park for a proposed Metro station, the local clerics sounded a warning: The park stood on a medieval era mosque built by Aziz-un-Nisa Begum or Akbarabadi Begum, one of the wives of Mughal emperor Shah Jahan. Aziz-un-Nisa hailed from the royal family of Agra and is said to have been seen by the emperor while plucking roses from her garden. He then proposed a matrimonial alliance. The mosque was torn down by the British after the First War of Independence in 1857, probably because a fatwa was issued by the clerics of the masjid, Shah Waliullah and Shah Abdul Aziz, against the British. The fatwa so infuriated the British that the mosque was razed to the ground, goes the story.

Akbarabadi Masjid was no ordinary mosque. Located barely a quarter mile from the majestic Jama Masjid, it was built by Akbarabadi Begum, who is said to have calmed her husband and tried to bring him to the path of religion after the loss of his favourite wife, Mumtaz Mahal. Incidentally, Aziz-un-Nisa herself was not too keen to move to Delhi from Agra, but did so out of respect for her husband's word. Once in Delhi, she decided to construct the said mosque with the idea that the emperor would have to pass through her mosque on his way to offer prayers at the much more majestic Jama Masjid. She, in fact, planned another mosque in Old Delhi's Pahari Bhojla area to rival the one built by her husband! The plan could not fructify though.

Akbarabadi Begum was a scholar of Islam. She had translated the Quran into Urdu while living near Jama Masjid, almost exactly at the spot where Akbarabadi Masjid stood. The masjid's construction, which began in 1650, was completed across two years. Once completed, its white marble dome and two lofty minarets seemed set on the pattern of the Jama Masjid nearby. Akbarabadi Begum continued to spend some time in a room[1] even after the mosque started functioning.

Akbarabadi Masjid was not the only mosque built by a woman from the royal harem at that time. It was common enough for royal women to fund the construction of prayer houses at that time. Many, in fact, came with fellow inmates of the zenana (ladies' section) of the royal household to offer salat in the masjid. This was done on special occasions, such as a new king gracing the throne or when a royal inmate had had a prayer answered.

A few brisk steps from Akbarabadi stood Matia Begum Masjid in Matia Mahal. Matia Begum too was a wife of the emperor Shah Jahan. Similarly, not too far from the emperor's residence was Zeenat-ul-Masjid, in what is now Daryaganj. It was constructed by Aurangzeb's daughter Zeenat-un-Nissa, who showed her inclination towards spiritual matters by building this mosque to the south of the grand old Red Fort in 1700. Now popularly known as the Ghata Masjid, it was used as a bakery for troops for many years after the failed First War of Independence. Today, it is the first mosque in the area to host the Friday prayers every week. Hundreds of men gather for the weekly prayer. However, no woman is seen at the masjid built by a woman. Even the old-timers believe that the mosque was built by a woman for the benefit of men in this world, and her own life in the Hereafter. Women are conveniently excluded from the here and now.

Mubarak Begum Masjid

Delhi has a unique mosque built by a woman who was once a Brahmin dancing girl in Pune. The girl converted to Islam and left her

---

[1] Based on my research for a piece I wrote for *The Statesman* in 1998.

old profession. Now known as Mubarak Begum, she married the British Resident in Delhi, General David Ochterlony. Thanks to her new-found status, she came to be called General Begum! Ochterlony was a much married man, and Mubarak Begum was his 13th matrimonial partner. Predictably, she outwitted other wives of the General and bore him two daughters, whom she raised as Muslim girls.

Mubarak Begum wanted to atone for the sins of the past and decided that constructing a mosque would be a good idea to improve her position on the scales of piety. Thus began the construction of Mubarak Begum's Masjid in Hauz Qazi area, a few steps from what is Delhi's Metro station. It was, and continues to be, a small mosque, roughly around 8 metres by 5 metres. Built with red sandstone, the mosque has shops on the ground floor, with the main prayer hall accessible by a flight of stairs.[2] The first floor has a big courtyard, visible to the naked eye from adjacent buildings and a prayer chamber with three segments. The main dome is disproportionately large for a small mosque. A plaque at the entrance gives its year of construction as 1823 and Mubarak Begum's full name as the patron, Bibi Mahruttun Mubarak-ul-Nissa Begum. She was said to have relinquished her early profession and even enrolled to go on the hajj pilgrimage. Incidentally, taking inspiration from her early years, sex workers of the modern GB Road, located at less than a kilometre from the mosque, used to come to watch films at New Amar Cinema in the vicinity. The cinema, keeping in mind their difficult life, often played women-centric films with a strong female character. It is said, back in the Emergency days, some sex workers got to know of the antecedents of the patron of the Mubarak Begum Masjid. Initially, they refused to believe. But once they were convinced, so inspired they were that they started collecting funds from their earnings to build another mosque. The fund-raising drive continued for about a year. Their efforts did not bear any fruit though. Today, most of them have retired from their profession and some have passed away. The cinema where they often met, New Amar,

[2] Based on my visit to the place.

has also been demolished to make way for a local metro station. The mosque stands safe and sturdy, as ever.

As for Mubarak Begum, her desire for pilgrimage, or entry into nobility, did not mean she stayed away from the politics of the day. She is said to have been a parallel power centre to her husband. Keen to move up in social station, Mubarak Begum often called herself Lady Ochterlony, much to the dismay of the British. With that nomenclature, she wished to get the approval of the ruling classes. Likewise, with the construction of the mosque, she wanted to win over the ulema.

For the locals though, her action of building a mosque failed to win any popular approval. Many derided the house of worship as *Randi ki Masjid* or the Prostitute's Mosque. Most, however, refrained from using the term, and called the place by the name of its builder. The uncharitable remarks about the Begum, however, did not prevent the faithful from coming to the mosque to offer their daily prayers. Today, local shopkeepers and residents use the mosque for their daily prayers as also the Friday congregation. Unfortunately, here also women are excluded from the mosque built by a woman. Never mind an illuminated board in the courtyard that reproduces part of a verse from Surah Nisa (Women)! It reads, 'Verily, prayers are enjoined on the believers at stated times.' The irony does not strike the men around. Like at most places in India, they tend to believe that only they are believers.

Fatehpuri Masjid, Chandni Chowk

The night of the new moon is a night of anticipation. Within minutes of sunset, queries start pouring in, 'Has the moon been sighted?' If not sighted within the city, calls are made to friends or relatives in neighbouring cities, 'Has the moon been sighted there?' It goes on for a couple of hours, or until the matter is decided one way or the other. Two nights are anticipated more than all nights put together. They are the night marking the commencement of Ramadan, the month of fasting, with the sighting of the new moon, and the night marking the completion of fasting, and ushering in of Eid. While Muslims all over

India wait for these two nights—it is pretty common to see children and adults alike standing on the roofs of their houses post sunset and straining their necks to see a sliver of the new moon—it is particularly crucial at the 17th century Fatehpuri Masjid, at the west end of Chandni Chowk. It is from here that the announcement of the new moon is made. Once the main imam Mufti Mukarram makes the announcement of the sighting of the new moon, it sends the city into a tizzy of activity.

On the eve of Ramadan, the faithful change into white kurta-pyjama and rush for Taraweeh. The masjid comes alive as men young and old take up every inch of space available. It remains that way almost the entire month. At the conclusion of the Quranic recitation, men walk home, spiritually elevated, and a packet of sweets in their hand. Women? As the initial tumult of the new moon subsides, they stay at home. Some pick up the Quran kept carefully in a velvet cover on the top shelf and start reading it. Most confine themselves to reading the Arabic text; a few go in for a translation of the same. Other women spread their prayer mats and get busy with their individual prayer for the next hour or so. Then, when the menfolk come back from the mosque, they eat together.

It has been so for more than a century. Men go to the mosque and women stay home. Fatehpuri Masjid, from where the announcement of the new moon is made, is no exception. Not just the Ramadan, even the sighting of the new moon for Eid does not change one bit for women. In the morning on Eid, men gather at the Fatehpuri Masjid; the mosque holds what is probably the earliest Eid prayer in Delhi. With men come a lot of boys, some of them too small to know their prayers. Occasionally, just occasionally, a few girls, who haven't hit puberty yet, run around the place in their new dress and offer prayers standing at the end of *saffs*.

This is true of most other mosques in India, yet here it hurts more. First, men monopolise the session in which they listen to the recitation of the Quran in Ramadan. Then on Eid, women stay at home, and men come out to pray, hug each other and celebrate. This happens in a mosque that was built by a Mughal princess! The mosque is named after Fatehpuri Begum, a consort of the Mughal emperor Shah Jahan who was with him during his years of imprisonment and stayed by his side till the end. A woman could build the mosque in 1650, but women cannot pray in the mosque in 2019. Such is the sorry state of affairs at this mosque with a large single dome and two minarets measuring up to 48 metres in height. At one time, the Mughal nobles emerging from the Red Fort would walk down Chandni Chowk and offer prayers at the Fatehpuri Masjid. The mosque used to have three gates; they are still extant, as the faithful believed in entering the mosque from one gate and departing from another. While Fatehpuri Begum lies forgotten in a tomb in Agra, and women continue to be banished from the mosque, Fatehpuri Masjid has a rich and chequered history. This mosque, known for its simplicity and precision in its arches and domes, fell into the hands of the British after the failed First War of Independence in 1857. The British closed the mosque for prayers. They instead used it to keep their horses. It was then auctioned by the British. It was bought by a local businessman Seth Chunamal for ₹19,000. It was only in 1877 that the mosque was repurchased from him in lieu of four villages, and the charge was given back to the Muslims. Till now the prayers have continued uninterrupted. The prayers are attended by men only. Women are seldom heard or seen, and never ever in a *saff* for group prayers.

However, a few women still come to this mosque every day, partly due to the mausoleum of a few Sufis within its precincts. These women belong to all religions and come to the mosque for a spiritual experience, some to find a solution to a nagging personal problem. While they take guidance from the imam or some other cleric every evening, some of them do offer their prayers just outside the imam's room. This is the only contact with women at the Fatehpuri Masjid in modern India. Otherwise, for all five prayers a day and then the special Friday prayers, Fatehpuri Masjid, despite its huge size, fails to find space for women. Amazingly, on one of its walls, the mosque guides the faithful to the correct way of establishing prayer.

The entire process is given and the verses of prayer are recalled. Men read and take heed. The rare women who can read head home and offer prayers. The mosque continues to be a male monopoly. It has been so ever since the locals can remember.

Taj-ul-Masajid, Bhopal

For more than a hundred years, Bhopal was ruled by women. It was an anomaly in a country that had witnessed the bloodiest wars of succession between the sons of a king after his departure. Except Razia Begum, until the 19th century, no woman had ascended the throne at the death of her father or even husband. Begum Qudsia Begum (1819–37) though blazed a new trail when she stood up for her fifteen-month-old daughter Sikandar at the death of her young husband.

Between Qudsia and Sultan Jahan Begum (1901–26), Bhopal was ruled by four extraordinary women. They ruled the princely state with a heavy hand, instilling discipline into the administration, commanding the army and even rallying the Islamic clerics in their favour. Qudsia Begum laid the foundation of this female dominance when at the condolence ceremony of her husband, she addressed the assembled men and women, stating her wish to protect the legacy of her family. She thereby declared her fifteen-month-old daughter Sikandar Begum as the heir. Extinguishing any possibility of a controversy later on, she got the Qazi and Munsif to acknowledge a woman's right to rule in Islam. Thus, she covered all the bases. In future, nobody could point out that the rule of the Begum was against the shariah; she had the Qazi, an Islamic judge's word to prove it. She thus became the first woman ruler in the entire South Asia who also had her legitimacy acknowledged by jurists of Islam. She also approached a British agent to legitimise her status as the ruler of Bhopal. The British being keen to keep the reins of power in the family of Dost Mohammed Khan agreed. Qudsia's husband Nawab Nazar Mohammad Khan hailed from the same dynasty. His death when Qudsia was merely eighteen or so meant that she had to step forward to rule. And rule Bhopal she did!

Bhopal flourished under the Begums. The fourth, Sultan Jahan Begum was a reformer and an educationist. She went on to be the Chancellor of Aligarh Muslim University. She also became the President of the *All India Muslim Ladies' Association*. Sultan Jahan Begum also sought to complete the construction of the world-famous Taj-ul-Masajid in Bhopal, the largest mosque in India. The construction was started by Shah Jahan Begum, her mother. However, Sultan Jahan Begum was unable to complete the task. In fact, a slew of development projects she started left the state treasury almost empty. The mosque's construction could only be completed after the Independence of India. It was resumed in fits and starts in the late 1950s. The construction remained halted for a few decades, before it was resumed in 1971 by Mohammad Imran Khan Nadwi and Maulana Syed Hashmat Ali. The mosque was completed only in 1985 when the eastern gate was renovated in a major way with ancient motifs from the Syrian mosques. The motifs were a gift of the Emir of Kuwait in the memory of his wife. Fittingly too, as the three-domed, two-minarets mosque's construction began under one woman and got completed in the memory of another woman.

Incidentally, the Begums of Bhopal funded the construction of the Shah Jahan Mosque in Surrey, England. It was built in 1889 and has space for women worshippers.

Yet the Bhopal mosque with a two-storeyed gateway and an elaborate water tank in the centre could never find designated space for women worshippers. The mosque continued to be talked of as the pride of Bhopal. The residents were never tired of singing the praises of their women rulers, often to impose an idea of their liberal upbringing. Yet the largest mosque the Begums built had no space for women. This is ironical considering the Begums demolished all stereotypes of their generations, including stepping out of purdah to assume power, riding horses and elephants, commanding the army and giving the state administrative reforms. They were well read, and one of them, Begum Nawab Sikandar, had a rare ability with the pen. She published an account of her pilgrimage to Makkah and Medina in Urdu. It was translated into English as *A Pilgrimage to Mecca*. However, her exposure to the Prophet's Mosque and Al-Masjid al-Haram failed to bring about a change in the male-dominated outlook prevalent at the Taj-ul-Masajid. The mosque, to this day, has no space for women; the occasional woman devotee who comes here has to offer her own individual prayer. She cannot think in terms of standing behind men or with her fellow women devotees in a *saff.* Women have never established prayer in a congregation here. No local person remembers seeing women come in groups to the mosque; the only time they find women here is when they come as curious tourists. They come having heard the tales of the dominance of the Begums of Bhopal. They often go back with stories of social stereotypes. Not surprisingly, the mosque, for many years, hosted the annual *ijtema*, the congregation of the conservative Muslim body, Tablighi Jamaat. The three-day *ijtema* used to draw huge crowds from across the world, with many coming in from Bangladesh and Pakistan besides Egypt and South Africa. Elaborate arrangements used to be made for their boarding and lodging. After all, they were considered pilgrims who had left the comfort of their homes to spread the word of Allah. Among the lakhs of visitors, there used to be no woman. It was an all-male *jamaat*, an all-male congregation comprising men dressed in pyjamas that ended above their ankles, head covered and long and luxuriant beards. Men came and read from *Fazail-e-Amaal*, the body's popular book of some authentic and some inauthentic Hadiths that they refer to for guidance. They did not often consult the Quran, leaving it to the ulema. No woman was permitted. It was nothing but the biggest irony in a mosque conceptualised and built by women rulers of the state.

The Begums never got a chance to pray here as the mosque was completed much after they had passed away. If they were alive today, they would have surely been shocked at the way the mosque has been monopolised by men.

Invite to the way of *your Lord* with wisdom and good instruction, and argue with *them* in a way that is best. Indeed, *your Lord* is most knowing of who has strayed.

—Surah Al-Nahl [verse 125]

CHAPTER 17

Women Taking the Lead

Farhat Hashmi

A world removed from most other women fighting for women's rights in Islam, Farhat Hashmi is the best qualified to speak on the subject. She holds a Ph.D in Islamic Studies from the University of Glasgow, Scotland. She has earlier been an assistant professor at the Faculty of Usul-al-Din at International Islamic University, Islamabad. Married to fellow academic-televangelist Idrees Zubair, she continues to use her maiden name.

She was probably the first woman scholar of the century to come up with a *tafsir*, commentary of the Quran. Hardly surprising, her website's slug goes, 'Quran for all—in every hand, in every heart'. Yet she, more than other reformers, has had to face the brunt of anger of the society, not just rigid clerics or egoist men, but even women, including those working for the upliftment of women, and winning their sacred space. Nobody has spared Hashmi. While the maulanas initially argued against a woman preaching, contending that as a woman the best she could do was to give right upbringing to her children, the traditional women, indoctrinated for centuries, repeated men's arguments. The progressive ones did not find her progressive enough. She did not challenge the male order, they alleged. She was happy with male imams; hence not quite the woman to challenge the social stereotypes. They insisted Hashmi sought no overhaul of the social order, but limited herself to the rights and responsibilities enshrined in the Quran.

Hashmi though reacted neither to the clerics nor the self-appointed feminists. She continues to do the same today. She concentrates her energies on bringing about a positive change, through a better understanding of the Quran. Shunning a confrontationist approach with respect to the larger patriarchal society, Hashmi seeks to inculcate in her women students a true understanding of their rights and—unlike many other women striving to bring about change—their responsibilities too. It is not uncommon for her to break a lecture on the *tafsir* on the Quran to add an everyday example. The example is usually taken from women's daily lives, like their marital relations, their duties as a mother, as a neighbour and so on. Where she stands out, she speaks to women in their language and delivers a sermon on the Quran like a doctor attending to patients. She is patient, calm, gentle and persuasive. She is almost like a doctor trying to prevail upon a habitual smoker to quit the bad habit.

A little more than a decade ago, Hashmi's classes started making waves, winning over many housewives initially and then the working women too. The classes in India were held by her erstwhile students; those who had gained from listening to her in Pakistan, Canada, the US and other places. Thus equipped, they came to Indian cities, such as Mumbai, Delhi, Jaipur, Patna and Hyderabad, to start Al-Huda Quran classes with the CDs of her lectures, her *tafsir* and her short sermons. Women in India, almost always neglected by Indian Muslim clerics, reacted positively. For the first time, somebody was speaking to them about true Islam, not speaking at them. For the first time, somebody told them to understand the Quran, go to the root of every word and see the text against the context in which it was revealed. As more and more women joined in and took home the lectures, the menfolk resisted—the clerics in particular. Some had the audacity to say that Hashmi was going against faith. Many argued,

> Dawah (invitation) is the not the job of a woman. Whatever she has to preach, she should confine herself to women close by. We do not approve of this CD and recording business. Aurat ki awaaz ka purdah hota hai (A woman's voice should remain under cover).

Clearly, they were rattled. In an age when a leading Muslim body like the Tablighi Jamaat with millions of members across the world had failed to come up with one *tafsir* of the Quran of international renown, here was a woman from Pakistan charting a path all on her own. She had no contemporary role models. She did not make lofty statements at press conferences against the male order or the clergy. Yet she shook the very basis of the patriarchal society by equipping women with the knowledge of the Quran. Further, at a time when most madrasas are still caught in a time warp and continue to resist technology, Hashmi used the latest technology in her study circles to get her sermons and commentary across to millions. While the best of sermons by an imam in a city were heard only by a few hundreds, or a thousand or two, Hashmi's word travelled far and wide through her students. Well-known writer Aneela Zeb Babar noted in her book *We Are All Revolutionaries Here*,

> Al Huda's 'living room seminaries' abroad (domestic spaces that hosted scripture groups) and the Al Huda campuses in Pakistan and abroad were these new emerging religious spaces that Pakistani women were either allowed to access, or they struggled to be allowed to them. From the networks they formed through their dars (lecture/scripture meetings), I could see these cities being mapped .... Women's dars meetings created religious and diasporic spaces 'previously non-locative' if I had looked them up in the street directory, reflecting the 'imagined maps of diaspora Muslims.' ... The Al Huda phenomenon is a road map to how Pakistani women negotiate ethnic social relations—whether they be belief systems, generational change, ethnicity, class, gender, sexuality, or whether they choose to veil or not. Al Huda is their positioning of the self .... Young Pakistani women like their sisters elsewhere in the

> Muslim world are building upon their interest in religious studies. Unlike their grandmothers who were content to read the Quran in Arabic (for many this was their only form of 'literacy'), they exhibit great enthusiasm about learning how to translate the Arabic of the Quranic verses. Not content with the traditional explanations of the Quranic verses offered to them by their mothers' generation, they explore alternative commentaries for their religious texts. This can be phrased as the 'engendering of religious literacy'.[1]

What Babar wrote about the women in Pakistan is true for the women in India as well.

Gradually, it was the use of technology that helped Hashmi scale the gender barrier. Her students, initially all women, took Hashmi's lectures at home on their iPods, mobiles and laptops. As part of their homework, they had to listen to the lectures. As more and more women listened at home, the menfolk gradually, almost grudgingly, even unwittingly came around. At home, they could not help but listen to Hashmi's lectures, playing alternatively in the bedroom and kitchen. After some time, men realised that whatever Hashmi taught was from the Quran. What's more, she did not raise her voice to make a point, unlike the neighbourhood maulanas who often resorted to loudness in lecture. Many felt sheepish at initially opposing their wives or daughters' move to attend the classes. Some went a step further. They started listening to the Quran *tafsir* by Hashmi themselves. Some played it in their car on their way to work and others on their long journeys. They all felt enlightened. Hashmi's way of expression, her analogies were remarkably different from the time-worn expressions used by sundry maulanas in mosques and madrasas. And the new-generation thinking men could identify with her.

Hashmi's classes developed into a silent social movement. Soon, working men joined in special classes. Most came on weekends, but

[1] Babar, Aneela Zeb. 2017. *We Are All Revolutionaries: Militarism, Political Islam and Gender in Pakistan.* New Delhi: SAGE and Yoda Press.

some also came in the evening after a hard day at work. All like the fact that modern tools of technology, such as projector, recorder, iPod, etc., were used. It was not like that when many of them had gone to a local madrasa in their childhood. It was Islam, the way it was preached by the Quran, which says, 'Rabbi zidni ilma' (O Lord, increase me in knowledge). The barriers had been removed. That too without Hashmi setting a foot in a class herself! She thus proved to be one of the most influential Islamic scholars of the century. Incidentally, this yearning to instil in her students, an ability to have a one-to-one understanding of the Quran, stems from Hashmi's upbringing. Daughter of Abdur Rehman Hashmi, a renowned Islamic scholar who instilled in her the desire to take forward the message of Allah, she realised early that when the Quran tells us, 'Invite them to Allah' (Surah Qasas [verse 87]) or 'Invite them to the path of Allah with words of wisdom and good instruction', the instruction is for both men and women. She undertook her responsibility, and without screaming her lungs out, she shook the established patriarchy.

Not everybody was convinced. She was dubbed a Wahabi or an agent for promotion of Saudi-brand of Islam. It is a charge she is used to facing. She said, in her typical non-confrontational way, on her website,

> I honestly did not know what a Wahabi is till I was labeled one! This is a typical example of labelling and stereotyping without authentic reason or proof. Personally, I can vouch for the fact that I have no affiliation with any religious group and I respect every Islamic scholar or group so long as they are in accordance with the Quran and Sunnah.

She added,

> There is nothing such as the Saudi, the Pakistani, the Eastern or the Western brand of Islam. Islam is for the entire humanity. Islam is not against geographical dispositions and culture, and neither am I.

> Any country's cultural inclinations and customs, so long as they don't clash with the Islamic rulings, are fine by me. The seed of Islam is the same, but the land you will plant it on will leave its flavor on it. As for Saudi Arabia, I have never got any special support from there. My allegiance is with Islam and Islam is a global religion and way of life.

Finally, almost inevitably, she was branded as a western agent of change, who was making women negligent of their duties as a homemaker or a mother. Refusing to be flustered, she said,

> Islam has given clear roles and rights to both males and females. Ignorance about Islam had lulled women into a semi-conscious state about their rights as women. Quranic awareness has just woken them up and brought certain issues to light. I do not have a gender-biased approach. As far as women coming to masjid for prayers is concerned, there is a not a single verse in the Quran preventing them from coming to masjid nor any authentic Hadith. But there are many Hadiths of the Prophet (pbuh) allowing women to go to the masjid. For instance, 'When your wives ask you to go to the mosque, do not prohibit them (Sahi Bukhari), or 'Do not prevent the servants of Allah from going to the mosque (Sahi Muslim) or 'Do not take away the share of the mosque of the women (Sahi Muslim).'

Clearly, Hashmi believes in a path uniquely her own. Unbowed in front of male dominance, she continues to defy the stereotypes of female liberation.

Amina Wadud

In July 2013, Amina Wadud, an African-American Muslim based in Maryland, was supposed to deliver a talk on 'Islam, Gender and Reform' at the Centre for Islamic Studies, University of Madras in Chennai. The topic was pretty appropriate for the speaker who had authored a book *Inside the Gender Jehad: Women's Reform in Islam*. The talk was to be followed by a roundtable discussion on Women's Experiences and the Questions of Authority in Islam.[2]

Wadud, it may be added, had arrived in India with many of the residents nursing misgivings with respect to her approach to Islam. With an independent mindset, Wadud had constantly urged the community members in the US and indeed in the other countries she had spent reasonable time in, such as Malaysia, Indonesia and Libya, to interpret the Quran in the light of emerging challenges. She had also, back in 2005, led a mixed gender prayer in New York, evoking extremes within the ummah.

The *imamat* of men and women alike in the Friday prayers was not a sudden decision foisted upon her by circumstances. It was a well-thought-out decision stemming from her belief that women enjoyed as much right to a mosque, and indeed to leading the prayers, as men. More than a decade before leading the prayers in Synod in New York, Wadud had travelled to South Africa. It was a tour that was to change her perspective of Islam. In 1994, she attended a conference on the rights of women in Islam in South Africa and was invited to give a khutbah (sermon) before the Friday prayers. Though it seemed a small step at that time, it proved to be a big leap in the inter-gender relations for the faithful. As she recalled in an interview a few years later,

> Both those who invited me and I knew that this was a landmark event because it could change the idea of Islamic leadership. From that moment, I spent ten years doing research, in order to better understand how women could become prayer leaders. Over the years, I understood the importance of equality in Islam. This is the reason why, in 2005, I accepted the invitation to lead a mixed prayer in the Synod House, New York. I wanted to prove that

[2] The talk was due to be held at the Department of Islamic Studies in July 2013, but was cancelled.

> human beings are on a horizontal line of reciprocity, that means that there is no role that is fixed by gender unless determined by biology.[3]

Gradually with her constant study, she came to the conclusion that the Muslim community was not living as per the teachings of the Quran. This, in turn, started a quest to understand women's role in Islam, culminating in leading the prayer—an action, she contends, that is not opposed by the Quran. 'The Quran never says that the imam cannot be a woman and must be a man. Whenever there is a difference in the interpretation, we have to use our intelligence to understand the real meaning of Islam.'

Her action, while warmly appreciated in a small section of American-Muslim society, attracted waves of criticism across the world, with ulema denouncing the mixed gender prayer as a mark of going astray. Though Wadud stuck to her guns, and often found herself flooded with requests for interviews at this silent churning within the circle of the faithful. She declined most of them, making an exception for Chennai.

For the locals, including those who opposed her decision to lead the prayers, and based their argument from Islamic history, the talk provided an excellent opportunity to cross-check the media reports by interacting with the lady at the centre of a storm. Just as Surah Hujurat, [verse 6] instructs, 'O you who have believed, if there comes to you a disobedient one with information, investigate, lest you harm a people out of ignorance and become, over what you have done, regretful.'

The talk, however, was cancelled at the last minute because some local residents protested against the opportunity given to Wadud to spread her ideology from a public platform. Their vehement protest resulted in the suspension/cancellation of the talk.

---

[3] Meringolo, A. 2013. 'Amina Wadud, Portrait of a Muslim Feminist'. Available at: https://www.resetdoc.org/story/amina-wadud-portrait-of-a-muslim-feminist/ (accessed on 25 April 2019).

This was not something Wadud had not experienced in varying degrees earlier. Before she led the prayers at Synod House at the Cathedral of St John, the Divine, in Manhattan, three mosques and an art gallery had turned down the proposal following threats to life.

Clearly upset at the way things had shaped up, Wadud, who had spent considerable time waiting at the Calicut Airport for a delayed flight to Chennai, left in a huff, stating, 'People of India, you have a chance to redeem yourselves for your own best interest. Do not be silent when the ignorant speak, claim your voice.'

It is a piece of advice that has still not been followed by a large section of the community. Men continue to deny women their space in the mosques. No verse from the Quran is quoted in defence. Worse, the text of Hadiths is quoted out of context.

It is particularly sad when one understands that Wadud is a reverted Muslim. She was born to a Methodist father who encouraged her to read and to ask questions. Her father emphasised the relation between God and justice—not too dissimilar from the teachings of the Quran. Wadud though was a follower of Buddhism. It was only after a sustained study of Islam that she decided that Allah was just and loved justice. Then in 1972, she embraced Islam. Living in a society where racial discrimination rears its head periodically, she was attracted to Islam's equality, specially the emphasis on racial and economic equality. Shortly after leading the prayers in 2005, she said,

> The relationship between God and justice is more articulated in Islam. This is one of the reasons why Islam had such great appeal to me. Social justice, gender equality, love, mercy and reciprocity between women and men are the inspiration I received from the Quran, and I will do everything I can to achieve this in the world.

Today, even as she advocates fresh interpretations of the Quran to face emerging challenges, she reiterates that all she aspires to do is to live her life like she is in the presence of the Divine every moment.

> I am inspired by the desire to live my life in a way where the presence of Allah is manifest in everything that I do. I am motivated to live a life with the consciousness of this sacred goal: returning to Allah, our origin point.

As for women seeking to use the Islamic permission to offer their prayers in the mosques, she says,

> I don't adhere to any notion that there is such a thing as a singular 'Islamic permission'. All of Islam, as it has been practiced and believed for a millennium and a half, was constructed on the basis of power and privilege (mostly male thinkers and believers). I can say this: Since no verse of the Quran prohibits women from leading, and no verse assigns or requires that men lead, and no Hadith or statement of the Prophet prohibits women from leading, and no statement requires that leaders be male, how did we get to that general consensus?

Jamida Beevi

Around the time Narendra Modi was aspiring to be the Prime Minister of India in 2014, little known Jamida Beevi was fighting a battle uniquely her own. Driven out of her home in Malappuram, Kerala, she made a living by teaching Arabic to a handful of students in Thiruvananthapuram. She organised complimentary Quran classes too. As she taught children in the morning and took Quran classes a little later in the day, Jamida presented an ideal figure of a pious woman devoted to the service of the Lord. Yet, there was little calm, almost no serenity. Her ability to ask uncomfortable questions did not stand the patriarchal society in good stead. Not only did she teach the Quran, Jamida also interpreted it her own way, turning many a long-held belief on its head. The first murmur of discontent came when she refused to say 'Amen' at the conclusion of Surah Fatiha, the opening verse of the Quran, so essential in nature that no prayer is ever complete without its recitation.

Jamida recited Surah Fatiha, like millions of others, but did not end it by saying 'Amen' or 'Ameen' (meaning, so be it) as people tend to do. Her argument, as a scholar of Arabic, being that the word 'Amen' is not an Arabic word. And since the entire prayer is in Arabic, a non-Arabic word affects the sanctity of the prayer. To her it makes perfect sense, but to a large section of believers, less so. The Muslim clerics were upset enough to even dub her an apostate.

Jamida though, remained unbowed, her argument being she was drawing solace from the Quran. And that Allah does not discriminate between men and women; it is the society that does.

Her fiercely independent take on religion, though shocking for the larger society, was not unexpected for those who knew her from close quarters. She was the youngest of the thirteen children of an Army soldier and pursued Arabic at Jamia Nadwiyya Arabic College in Malappuram. Right from the initial days, she stood out as someone who did not shy away from questioning long-held beliefs. Usually, in her quest for answers, she ran into a wall. As she told scroll.in in an interview in 2018,[4]

> I was an inquisitive student ... I used to trouble my teachers with questions on Islam. My intention was to gain knowledge, but teachers misunderstood and called me a rebel. At times, teachers asked me not to enter the class as punishment. But I was adamant to know the truth. And my quest continues even now.

This endless quest for truth took Jamida to Quran Sunnat Society in the town. Even as she sought support from the Quran Sunnat Society, she continued her search for more knowledge of Islam. Soon, she came to the conclusion that Islam does not discriminate between men and women; it is the men who do. And that the Quran does

[4] Ameerudheen, T. 2018. 'Meet Jamida Beevi, the First Muslim Woman to Lead Friday Prayers in India'. Available at: https://scroll.in/article/866794/meet-jamida-beevi-the-first-muslim-woman-to-lead-the-friday-prayer-in-india (accessed on 25 April 2019).

not specify the gender of the imam. To her mind, an imam (one who led the prayer) could be a man or a woman. Knowledge of the verses of the Quran was essential, but gender was immaterial. She took the next step: she started leading women in the special Taraweeh prayers in the month of Ramadan. In the Taraweeh prayers, often the entire Quran is recited across the month. Jamida led the prayers. It upset not a man as only women prayed behind her initially. Then she did the unthinkable, something that had never been done in India since the time Islam came to the country in 629 AD with the establishment of the first mosque, Cheraman Juma Masjid in Thrissur district of Kerala. No woman had ever led men in prayer. Further, no mixed gender prayers had ever been reported. The mosques that did allow both genders to pray kept clearly specified spaces for men and women. Not so for Jamida. On Republic Day in 2018, she hit the headlines by leading a mixed gender group for the Friday prayers inside a hall in Kerala's Vandoor village in Malappuram district. She said the khutbah, as an imam does in a mosque, then led the prayers. There was a difference in prayer though. Instead of the usual two prostrations per cycle, she prostrated only once. And while getting up from the *rukuh* position (the time one stands with hands on knees before going down in prostration), Jamida did not say 'Sami'Allahu liman hamidah' (Allah hears whosoever praises Him). Instead, she said, Allah-o-Akbar (God is great) while getting back to the standing position. All this was contrary to how the prayer is performed across the world.

Speaking to *Frontline*, the thirty-four-year-old Jamida contended,

> I do things only according to the Quran. The Quran does not talk of two prostrations. So I do only one sajda (prostration). The phrase 'Sami'Allahu liman hamidah' is not from the Quran. I follow the Quran. Nothing else. I feel that in Hadith a lot of interpolations were made by men. Not every Hadith which has reached us is authentic. The Quran is original. Not a word has changed since it was revealed more than 1,400 years ago. I follow the Quran.

Incidentally, the methodology of the prayer comes from the practice of the Prophet; the Quran does not explain the way in which a prayer is to be offered. It only talks of the time of prayer.

Jamida's move called for widespread criticism. She took it as a sign that things were changing, that the patriarchal society was affected enough to react. Giving credit to P.K. Mohammed Abul Hassan, popularly known as Chekannur Maulavi—a progressive Islamic cleric who founded the Quran Sunnat Society and disappeared in 1993 under mysterious circumstances, only for the Central Bureau of Investigation (CBI) to conclude in 2010 that he had been murdered, possibly following accusations of being an apostate—Jamida insisted that she was not introducing a new thing in religion. That she was only following the Quran, and men were upset because women were feeling empowered due to her actions.

This is in a country where a vast majority of mosques have zero provisions for women. Did she realise she was leading prayers in a country where women, particularly in north and west India, are often not allowed in mosques? Asked to comment on the anomaly, she said,

> In 1922, when the Kerala Muslim Eikya Sangam was formed [the Nadwatul Mujahideen was formed in 1950 under the Kerala Jamiathul Ulama], they were the ones who first said that women can go to the mosque. Later, they said it was compulsory for them to go to the mosque. Then they said that women had the permission to go to the mosque. After that they took a stand that it was not compulsory. The prevailing stand is that it is not necessary. They believe that if women enter the mosque, that will violate its sanctity. That is the situation today .... They are trying to control women, treating them as second-class citizens. They want women to accept whatever they dole out (*audaaryam*) as freedom. This is the Islamic priests' decision; the power of the priests. They are against any advancement of women. That's why they came to the decision to not allow women to enter mosques and keep them out of leadership roles.

> The clerics do not go by the Quran in all the instructions they give. They often do not know what is in the Quran. They go by Hadith. They cite 'charitra rekhakal' [historical documents] to say 'good' women should not go to the mosque, they are better off praying at home. For them, women with a sound moral character pray at home. They often quote a Hadith that a woman's best prayer is in the innermost room of the house. But they have no evidence from the book [the Quran] in their favour. The Quran is the only solid evidence. And it addresses believing men and believing women, not just men. The Quran does not prohibit women from going to a masjid.

Soon after the incident, Jamida had to switch off her phone to avoid unwelcome callers. It became worse with not-so-subtle threats to life. She admitted,

> Plenty of messages have been circulating on social media alleging that I am a kafir, a non-believer .... Last week, someone sent me an image with my head fixed to a dead body. I see it as a warning .... I am not afraid of death. I am ready to die for the cause.

The phone stays switched off. Jamida remains incommunicado.

V.P. Zuhra

Daughter of a Muslim League politician from Kerala, Zuhra did not set out to be an imam. Even her demand for women to pray in the mosque, or to lead a prayer, came by the way. All she wanted to do was help Muslim women in distress, some victims of instant triple talaq, some being denied a share in the ancestral property and some looking for funds for higher studies. However, the Supreme Court verdict on Sabarimala, allowing women of all ages to enter the temple in Kerala, changed her perspective. The verdict was warmly welcomed by women even as political parties, such as the Bharatiya Janata Party and the Congress, urged the court to revisit the judgement. The judgement had its impact on women across religious divides. In the wake of the judgement, some Hindu women sought access to the prayer hall at the Vavar Mosque at Erumely en route to Sabarimala. Then, there were Muslim women led by V.P. Zuhra, who until then was busy piloting her Kozhikode-based body Nisa—meaning women, the name is derived from a Surah of the Quran—and was content with her social welfare activities. The verdict spurred her on to demand access to all the mosques for Muslim women. Further, like Jamida, she sought leadership roles for women in prayer, questioning the centuries-old practice of a man leading the prayers. Stepping away from the Islamic tradition and the Sunnah of the Prophet, Zuhra contended it amounted to discrimination against women. It may be reiterated that around 600 mosques affiliated to either Jamaat-e-Islami Hind or the Ahl-e-Hadith sect in Kerala welcome women and provide them the facilities needed for prayer. Zuhra wanted the same in all mosques. She resolved to approach the Supreme Court for redressal even as the patriarchal clergy sought to limit the access of women to the mosques. It became a tussle in Kerala towards the end of 2018, with women led by Zuhra seeking to become imams in mosques and the clergy seeking to limit their participation in the mosques.

In an interview with *Frontline*[5] Zuhra stated, 'We cannot be denied. Like men, we too have a constitutional right to offer prayer. We want access to all mosques of all denominations, not just a handful of mosques,' she said.

Significantly, this right is already safeguarded by Islam. The Prophet, too, never prohibited any woman from going to the mosques. The little difference of opinion between Caliph Umar and his wife on the subject is well documented. Equally well known is the caliph's refusal to stop her as it was a practice approved by the Prophet. The Prophet had actually asked men not to stop their wives

---

[5] Salam, Z. 2019. 'Leap of Faith'. Available at: https://frontline.thehindu.com/cover-story/article26003691.ece (accessed on 25 April 2019).

from going to mosques if they so desired. To a question regarding this, Zuhra replied:

> That is true, but Sunni men do not want to do that. Not just here, but across the world there are two important sects of Muslims, Sunni and Shia. While Shias allow women in mosques, Sunnis do not. We plan to fight this exclusion of women by Sunnis. Despite the injunctions in the Quran, they want to keep women under house arrest. They want to control women, and so this move to deny them the right to pray in a mosque. But we do not just want permission from men to go to a masjid. It is the right of women to go to a market, a masjid, everywhere. We want to enter mosques, but we will not limit ourselves to that. We want to be imams and to lead prayers. So far, only men have led prayers and women have stayed at the back.

Contrary to her claims, women do not have regular *jamaat* in most Shia mosques either. So, it is not a Sunni-specific exclusion.

She urged that women be allowed in the prayer hall of the Vavar Mosque too. Incidentally, Vavar is believed to have been a companion of Lord Ayyappa. Sabarimala pilgrims visit the mosque to offer prayers or perform rituals, such as circumambulation or breaking the coconut. The Vavar Mosque regularly receives women visitors and has not had any restriction on the entry of women or in performing the rituals according to tradition.

Zuhra plans to take the movement forward. She said:

> The Jamaat [Jamaat-e-Islami Hind] permits women to only go to a masjid. But they try to control women by insisting on purdah for small girls and by not permitting girls to take up a job. Women should be permitted to take up a job, enter a masjid and even be an imam. Now *imamat* is limited to men. This is not correct and we want to get the right to imamship for women also.

Though she plans to go to the Supreme Court for women's right to enter all mosques, Zuhra's journey has been far from easy. In the absence of support from her family, she has fought the battle all by herself. In mid-2018, she was subjected to online abuse. Apparently, posters were put up in the market near her residence with her photograph and a message that read, 'This is the person who wants to enter the masjid. Hope Allah calls her immediately.'

Zuhra was unmoved by the threat. In an interview she said,[6]

> This is not the first time that we are facing such threats. Since we are a progressive organisation, speak our minds and fight for our rights, we have always been receiving threats. Speaking for the rights of women is always dangerous, and you hardly get any support here. My family hasn't and never will support me in my endeavour. They are also against me filing a police complaint against the cyber attacks. They'll be more than happy to see us getting attacked. All this will not stop me from approaching the Supreme Court demanding the entry of women into the mosques.

Sabarimala has clearly inspired the likes of Zuhra.

Asra Nomani

'I think the Prophet would weep if he saw the injustices that women face today. Instead of progressing, we have gone backwards. I firmly believe it's critical for us to go back to the progressive values of Islam in the seventh century.' These are the words of fearless activist Asra Nomani, the US-based Islamic activist of Indian origin. Not long ago, she helped Amina Wadud become the first woman imam since the time of the Prophet to lead the Friday prayers. A little before that, she ruffled a few feathers by recounting her struggle to perform hajj, an obligation for all Muslims blessed with health and wealth, as a single woman.

[6] Abraham, K. 2018. Available at: https://www.thenewsminute.com/article/online-abuse-wont-stop-us-demanding-entry-women-mosques-says-kerala-activist-90055 (accessed on 25 April 2019).

Unlike most activists who quote from the West in their bid to bring about equality between genders, Nomani goes all the way back to the time of the Prophet, the time when his wives led prayers for fellow women and the time the Prophet's youngest wife, Ayesha, helped in recalling and recording the sayings of the Prophet after he had left this world in 632 AD. In fact, much of the Hadith that we have today have reached us through Ayesha. She says,

> Muslim women of the 7th Century had it better than many Muslim women of the 21st Century. Women prayed in the mosque of the Prophet Muhammad, while throughout India today women are barred from even entering many mosques. Women weren't required then to veil their faces. Now it is different.

Indeed, Nomani is a rare being, almost an endangered species: an Islamic feminist who takes recourse to the scriptures of the religion, the traditions of Prophet Mohammed and the Glorious Quran to vindicate her stand. This spirit of inquiry started early in her life. As she recalls,

> I was raised in a family in which my parents both valued the concept of independent and critical thinking. My father, Zafar Nomani, educated at Osmania University before coming to the United States, was a scientist, and he valued intellectual questioning. My mother, Sajida Ansari, before her marriage to my father, grew up in the hill station of Panchgani, outside Pune, and she went to a Catholic girls' school, where her teachers were nuns. All religions, including the Catholic faith, are hamstrung with sexism and dogmatism, but by being exposed to Christians so deeply, my mother asked herself questions that challenged the teachings the local maulana tried to teach her.
>
> My aha moment about the injustice of men's rules against women in Muslim society came when I was 11, in the fall of 1976, when I walked through the doors of graduate student housing on the campus of West Virginia University, off Van Voorhis

> Boulevard, in my hometown of Morgantown, West Virginia. As a young student from Hyderabad, I had arrived in the United States some years earlier as a four-year-old girl, living with my parents and older brother, Mustafa, in New Jersey, before we moved to West Virginia. I was a precocious but polite girl, eager to ask challenging questions, running with my full stride on our local track team and enjoying life, with spirit. In New Jersey, I had asked my mosque Sunday school teacher, Dr. Mahmoud Tahir, a kind man from Egypt, why we didn't assign prophet status to women in Islam. He eagerly discussed the question with me. I so appreciated it. And at our Muslim community picnics, we enjoyed our time together as families, in the same space.
>
> When I walked into the graduate student housing in West Virginia that night as a girl, I was excited to celebrate Eid-al-Adha. The night before, I had celebrated the Hindu festival of lights, called Diwali, in the same apartment complex. 'The party was short, but fun (playing),' I wrote into my journal, as a girl. I was hopeful for similar evening of energy and joy, as I stepped inside with my family in our best Eid clothes. I was in for a rude awakening. 'It stunk!' I wrote. 'The ladies had to go up to the little efficiency apartment.' I continued that 'they weren't to do this with men.' There were like 15 people in one dinky room! The men carried the food up and oh! It was as if we were in jail.
>
> As a girl, I discovered the second-class status that so many of us internalize and experience as girls and women in too many Muslim communities. The sexist interpretations of Islam put forth by the clerics of Saudi Arabia had spilled over into my little community in West Virginia. It was as a girl that I realized that men's interpretations of Islam had betrayed women and girls.

That set off a chain of events, leading Nomani to finally campaign for free and equal access to mosques for women. She urged women to even lead the prayers that included men.

> Islam had a progressive spirit that improved the rights of women and girls in the 7th Century tribal society around Makkah and

> Madina. That's how I choose to look at the black-and-white inequality and advocate for that progressive spirit to continue today into the 21st Century so that women and girls have equal rights to men and boys.
>
> When did we start the downward slide, away from progression? Immediately after the death of the prophet Muhammad, when women's and girls' rights were eroded, so that a culture of gender apartheid became normalized and is today the law in countries like Iran and the custom in too many communities, including in India.

Talking of India, Nomani takes heart from the effort of Tamil Nadu-based Daud Sharifa who tried to build the first women's mosque in the country.

> I am so heartened by women in India, like Sharifa who had a dream to create a women's mosque, because women were so often being unjustly treated after decisions about their lives were made by clergy and 'elders' in mosques. They were banned from entering mosques. I traveled to her home in Thandeeswara, Tamil Nadu, and I was so inspired by the women who traveled for hours for a meeting of their elders and youth council. I visited the mosque that she was attempting to build, brick by brick, beside vast rice paddy fields and dirt roads. I realized with their courage that we can all be courageous, challenging injustice that bars women from mosques and other rights in society. And that is what we must all do. We must say, 'No!' In our families, our communities, our towns, our lives, whenever we see a girl or a woman denied the rights that a boy or man receives.

Many years ago, she talked of Umm Waraqa as an inspiration. There are scholars of Islam who believe she led the prayers only for women or at best her family. Nomani disagrees,

> There is a consensus among even conservative scholars that Umm Waraqa led her family and local community in prayer, including

> a boy and an elderly man. The conservatives dispute the boy and elderly man equal the virile men they think they are (joke). To me, and others who believe in the right of women and girls to lead men and boys in prayer, who cares about virility? The point of the sunnah is that someone of a female gender led others of male gender in prayer. Why does it matter? Because the ban on women as imams is an extension of the second-class status we get in a culture of gender apartheid. Boys with runny noses can lead their mothers in prayers, but the wise mother cannot even lead her snotty-nosed son in prayer? We have to use commonsense and empower women and girls to be leaders in our society. Or is that the men who resist this progress are afraid of the competition?

Nomani though is ready to take on the patriarchal mindset head-on. As she said in an interview with *Frontline*, 'They use religion as an excuse to hold on to their power, and they must search deep within themselves to realise that we are serving humanity when we uplift all people, including women and girls.'[7] Then the prayer of Umm Waraqa in the 7th century came to her mind and she thought, 'Why not now?'

The quest is on.

[7] Salam, Z. 2016. 'From the Mosque to the Bedroom, We Must Assert Our Rights'. Available at: https://frontline.thehindu.com/cover-story/from-the-mosque-to-the-bedroom-we-must-assert-our-rights/article8523693.ece (accessed on 25 April 2019).

The world had heard the song of Unity from this place; The Leader of Arabia had felt a cool breeze from this place. That is my native land. That is my native land.

—Mohammed Iqbal

CHAPTER 18

Beyond Mosques

Haji Ali Dargah

Life had not been particularly kind to Fayyazi Begum. Married in her teens, she gave birth to two children, a daughter and a son, before her husband passed away. Widowed in the prime of youth, she married again. This time to her husband's younger brother as was the custom in many families in the Punjab, Awadh and Rajasthan region. She was blessed with another son. Not long after, her second husband died too, leaving Begum with three little children to bring up. She could only provide them basic education. And when her daughter came to a marriageable age, Begum did not take too long to finalise a matrimonial alliance for her. With her elder son also into teenage, Begum decided she had had enough of the mundane responsibilities of life. From the princely township of Rampur in western Uttar Pradesh, she came to Delhi and visited her daughter once to ascertain she was doing well. Soon after, she started on the longest journey of her life, a trip to the famous Haji Ali Dargah. Though not quite forty then, she decided to spend the rest of her life in prayer.

In Rampur, she had never entered a mosque, but at the Dargah she realised what it meant to pray with her sisters. She also understood what it meant to soak in the atmosphere at a mosque—the dargah is within the mosque. Located on an island off the coast of Worli in Mumbai, the Dargah was constructed in 1431. It was built in the memory of a rich merchant Syed Haji Ali Shah Bukhari, who hailed from Bukhara in Uzbekistan. A widely travelled man, he finally settled in Bombay, not far from the present Dargah. It is believed that the saint asked his followers not to bury him at any proper place or graveyard but they should drop his shroud in the ocean. The saint's wish was respected by his followers. Today, the Dargah is built at the same place where the shroud came to rest in the middle of the sea.

As for Begum, she spent the last few years of her life in peace and quiet. A few occasions when her family visited her to persuade her to come back home sufficed to tell her they were doing well. Begum stayed at the Dargah till her last breath, helping out with the maintenance of the premises, praying regularly and making sure that the love of worldly pleasures never entered her heart. Nobody knows where she is buried, if at all. For all one can guess, she might have opted for a water burial, just to be lowered into the sea, hoping the world forgets her.

Well, the world may have forgotten Begum, but people of all faiths continue to visit the Dargah. Here for centuries people have been allowed to visit the tomb of the saint. What is more, until 2011, women could actually come, touch and feel the place. There was nothing to distinguish a woman's visit from that of a man. It had been that way for around 500 years. Men and women visited the tomb, spent a few minutes in solitude and departed. Then, one not-so-fine day, a new board of trustees of the Dargah decided that the place could offer only limited access to women. Women could not visit the Dargah because of the stereotypical belief that they were impure, while others highlighted the fact that women were not allowed in a cemetery and the tomb was no different. In March 2011, a grill was put up beyond which women could not go to the Dargah. Many took it in their

This Much and No Further: Women are part of festivities and rituals at Nizamuddin Dargah but are denied access to the innermost chambers

stride, as they were used to being excluded from most mosques too. Some did not. They approached the board for redress. It did not work. They approached a couple of women's bodies. It proved futile. Then a group from the members of the Bharatiya Muslim Mahila Andolan (BMMA) went to the Dargah. The members were barred from entering the sanctum sanctorum. It led to an uproar. Women decided to pursue the matter. To some, this denial of entry was an infringement of the rights conferred by the Constitution, to others it went against Islam's spirit of equality. They were united in their belief that this stemmed from a patriarchal mindset, where men decided what women could do and how far they could go even in matters of worship. Soon, a campaign 'Haji Ali for All' started, and several women's groups, including the Bhumata Brigade, attempted to enter the premises. They were thwarted by the police.

The BMMA volunteers went to the Bombay High Court, which in August 2016 ruled in their favour even as it gave the Dargah's board time to make provisions for women to enter the premises from a specific pathway. It was stated in an article by legallyindia.com,

> In a historic verdict, the Bombay high court today permitted the entry of women up to the restricted grave area of the famous Haji Ali Dargah, located on the rocks off the Worli seashore. The ruling by a division bench comprising Justice VM Kanade and Mohite Revati-Dhere came in a Public Interest Litigation (PIL) filed by NGO Bharatiya Muslim Mahila Andolan and activists Noorjehan Niaz and Zakia Soman in November 2014. The PIL had challenged a move by the Haji Ali Dargah Trust prohibiting women from entering the sanctum sanctorum of the shrine, built in 1431. The shrine comprises the grave of Pir Haji Ali Shah Bukhari, a Muslim saint revered by all communities. While permitting women to enter the restricted areas along with men, the court asked the Maharashtra government to ensure their safety and security.[1]

On 26 August 2016, when the High Court said the ban on the entry of women into sanctum sanctorum contravened Articles 14, 15 and 25 of the Constitution, BMMA co-founder Noorjehan Safia Niaz said, 'Our faith in the Constitution has been established and affirmed by the HC order.' She added, 'Religious groups have always had a stranglehold and followed a patriarchal system. Our victory in this case was symbolic of the fact that we are equal citizens and equal Muslims.'[2] Her co-founder Zakia Soman expressed the hope that the Haji Ali verdict will pave the way for women's victory in Sabarimala too. 'We hope this case will also help in the Sabarimala temple case as it has a lot of public opinion around it as well,' said Soman. It was only in October 2016 that the Supreme Court declared that women could enter the sanctum. The

[1] IANS. 2016. 'Landmark: Bombay HC Opens Haji Ali Dargah to Women'. Available at: https://www.legallyindia.com/the-bench-and-the-bar/landmark-bombay-hc-opens-haji-ali-dargah-to-women-20160826-7924 (accessed on 25 April 2019).

[2] Shelar, J. 2018. 'Haji Ali Verdict Has Helped Us Feel Equal'. Available at: https://www.thehindu.com/news/cities/mumbai/haji-ali-verdict-has-helped-us-feel-equal/article24795290.ece (accessed on 25 April 2019).

Haji Ali Dargah Trust, which initially resisted women's entry after a ban was put in place in 2011–12 and had filed an appeal before the Supreme Court, conceded in October 2016 that women could enter the sanctum.[3] In November 2016, the volunteers of BMMA re-entered the Dargah, this time finding no obstacles in their path.

The decision, however, failed to settle an ongoing debate in the Muslim circles. Many argued against the Dargah itself while others to the presence of women. The former stated that Islam prohibits decorating the last resting place. It warns, as many believe, against building tombs to avoid setting up parallel places of worship as the faith is strictly about the worship of one God who has no equal, the One who begets not, nor was He begotten. It is under this light that the graves of the Prophet, his wives and companions are not covered with stones. In India, the last great Mughal emperor, Aurangzeb, said to be deeply religious, preferred that his grave be without ornamentation. Then, there are others who believe that women are not allowed to visit the graves as they are emotionally fragile. Some even believe they are even seen without clothes by the dead!

Others countered,

> Women are allowed to pay their respects at the graves of the Prophet's companions. Anybody who goes for Hajj or Umra visits the last resting place of the Prophet and two of the caliphs buried in the same compound. The men too recite Quranic verses at the graves of the departed, including the graves of the Prophet's wives.

The Supreme Court order, however, did settle the debate for women desirous of offering their prayers at the Dargah. For many men, it meant obeying the law of the land irrespective of their interpretation of the religious injunctions.

---

[3] Modak, S. 2018. 'Haji Ali: Two Years on, Women Entering Inner Sanctum Freely'. Available at: https://indianexpress.com/article/cities/mumbai/mumbai-haji-ali-dargah-women-entering-inner-sanctum-sabarimala-supreme-court-5408259/ (accessed on 25 April 2019).

Sabarimala

The Vavar Palli in Kottayam district of Kerala sends out a strong message of inclusiveness every year. The millions of pilgrims, who go to Sabarimala during the auspicious period beginning November, visit the mosque to offer prayers or perform rituals, such as circumambulation or breaking the coconut. It might sound strange to those not familiar with the local culture, but this mosque is named after Vavar, a companion of Lord Ayyappa. The mosque receives women visitors regularly and has not had any restrictions on the entry of women for performing the rituals according to their tradition.

Hailing the religious harmony and the message of gender equality emanating from the mosque, *The Indian Express*[4] noted,

> This is not a fairy tale of religious harmony but a real-life scene in Kerala where pilgrims of the famed Sabarimala Lord Ayyappa Temple visit a mosque and church as part of the annual Mandalam-Makaravilakku pilgrimage. Both the Erumeli Nainar Juma Masjid, also known as Vavar Palli (mosque), in Kottayam district and Arthunkal St Andrew's Basilica in neighbouring Alappuzha have been opening (their) portals for the devotees of Lord Ayyappa for decades during the two-month-long pilgrim season beginning in mid-November. Wearing the traditional black dress and bead-chain and smearing 'bhasmam', the holy ash, on forehead, chest and arms, Hindu pilgrims visit the mosque and the church every year and offer prayers, reviving the local myth of the Lord Ayyappa's friendship with a Muslim youth and a Christian priest.

According to Hakim, joint secretary, Erumeli Mahalla Muslim Jama-ath, not only Keralites but also devotees from neighbouring states of

[4] PTI. 2018. 'When a Hindu Deity's Muslim-Christian "Friendships" Set a Pilgrim Tradition in Kerala'. Available at: https://indianexpress.com/article/india/when-a-hindu-deity-muslim-christian-friendships-set-a-pilgrim-tradition-in-kerala-5485422/ (accessed on 25 April 2019).

Tamil Nadu, Karnataka and Andhra Pradesh visit the Vavar Mosque, situated over 60 kilometres from Sabarimala, every year and offer prayers before they start trekking the hill shrine. He said,

> A large number of Ayyappa pilgrims visit the mosque throughout the November–January annual pilgrim season. They do not enter the prayer hall but circumambulate the mosque, provide kanikka (offering) and break coconut at the premises. It is beautiful to see when we perform namaz inside the hall, our Hindu brothers perambulate the mosque and offer prayers as part of their traditional believes. The legend of the friendship of Ayyappa and Vavar is the reflection of the deep-rooted secularism and communal harmony in Kerala.

'The Jamaath, which takes care of the administration of the centuries-old mosque, provides parking facilities and space for placing "viri" (bed spread) for the "Ayyappas", how the Sabarimala pilgrims are generally known as.'

The story of the Vavar Mosque came as a much-needed balm as there was a huge controversy around the entry of women of all ages to the Sabarimala Temple throughout the winter of 2018–19. In September 2018, the Supreme Court threw open the doors of the hugely popular temple to women of all ages, including women in the menstruating age, between ten and fifty. The decision took many orthodox elements by surprise as they reckon Lord Ayyappa is a celibate deity, and the worshippers also have to observe the norms of celibacy for forty-one days. With women of menstruating age, it was not possible they argued. Even as the State was thrown into a state of turmoil many women welcomed the judgement as a landmark in gender parity. The fact that they could pray to the deity without having to wait for post-menstrual age meant there was no gender discrimination anymore. The deity was as accessible to them as he was to men. However, not everybody was pleased. There were right wing forces that read in the verdict an attempt to tamper with tradition. The President of the Bharatiya Janata Party Amit Shah said,

> I want to tell the (state) government and those who pronounce orders in court that you should issue orders that can be implemented, not the ones that break the faith of people ... Article 14 (right to equality) is always being cited and appreciated. But there are Articles 25 and 26 which give every citizen the right to follow his faith. How can one fundamental right subsume the other?

In the face of constant threats from the right wing forces against allowing any women in the compound, Kerala witnessed a historic show of unity among women cutting across barriers of caste and faith. Barely three months after the highest court's verdict, women brought together by the ruling Left Democratic Front in association with 172 social and caste organisations formed a 620 kilometre-long, largely unbroken, peaceful chain. Coming together under the banner of the Navodhana Mulya Samrakshana Samithi, the chain included women from all walks of life. The disciplined protestors took a pledge to fight for 'gender equality, secularism and the protection of values of Kerala's early renaissance movements'. Within hours of the conclusion of this chain, two women, Bindu Ammini (forty-two) and Kanakadurga (forty-four), entered the shrine with their faces covered and supported by policemen in plain clothes. With those few steps, they took a giant leap for the issue of gender justice. Their action though was greeted with dismay in some quarters. Amidst calls for observing Black Day against the State Government's decision to follow the Supreme Court order, there were rumours that more women, up to twenty had entered the temple for darshan after Ammini and Kanakadurga. Following the visit of the women, however, the priest of the temple immediately closed the sanctum sanctorum for an hour-long purification ritual. The ritual is usually performed after any act of defilement that affects the sanctity of the temple.

Though the Sabarimala Temple came back to public consciousness after the Supreme Court's verdict with several women's organisations hailing the judgement for being a landmark in gender justice, the temple has not always been closed to women. In fact, right from the time of Independence, through much of the 1950s and 1960s, it was a little known place, a temple located deep inside a forest and hence regarded outside of the Brahmanical tradition. The temple, as reported in *Frontline*[5]

> used to be visited in the olden days by people belonging to various tribes such as Malampantaram, Ullatar, Mannan and Narikkuravar, and a few low caste people settled along the fringes, besides some pilgrims from Tamil Nadu, annually during the Makara Sankramana (January–February). This tradition continued until recent times, accounting for the present claim of tribal heritage of the temple. In mid-June 1950, some poachers burnt the shrine and broke the idol of Ayyappa. For about a decade, the shrine remained in ruins, although the pilgrimage continued as usual. A new temple was constructed under the Travancore Devaswom Board (TDB), which was constituted in 1949–50 after the dissolution of the Travancore Royal Devaswom Commission. Ever since, there has been a steady rise in the number of pilgrims. The pilgrim traffic rose from a few hundred to several thousands in the 1970s and 1980s. In the 1990s, the flow of pilgrims became phenomenal, most of them drawn from the lower middle class of Tamil Nadu, Karnataka and Andhra Pradesh. In the process, the temple and the pilgrimage, once associated with the tribal peoples and lower castes, became completely overtaken by upper caste beliefs, institutions, customs and practices.

With increased inflow of pilgrims, the temple's coffers became much richer. Many millions of rupees and kilograms of gold reach the

---

[5] Gurukkal, R. 2019. 'Manufactured Legends'. Available at: https://frontline.thehindu.com/cover-story/article26002040.ece (accessed on 25 April 2019).

temple annually, turning the temple into a major business centre. Importantly, till the early 1990s men and women both enjoyed unrestricted access to the temple and the deity. In 1991, the High Court stipulated an age range of ten and fifty to disqualify women. The presumption being it would not be possible for them to observe forty-one days of penance due to their monthly menstrual cycle. It was based on the belief that Ayyappa, considered celibate, would not like young women visiting him. It is this presumption that was questioned by many women, who argued that in today's time it is possible to delay the onset of the menses with medicines. They scoffed at the idea of celibacy, asking if the deity could be susceptible to temptation. It was also pointed out that in Hinduism, in many sects the onset of puberty is celebrated as a sacred occasion. They also argued that the High Court judgement of 1991 was a proof that women had always enjoyed unrestricted access to the deity. *Frontline* observed,

> Several men, who go to Sabarimala as pilgrim tourists, are not even aware of the tradition of observing 41 days of penance, and hardly do they take celibacy and consumption of vegetarian food seriously. Many of them follow their own norms: they follow their own dress colour; some wear ochre-hued clothes, some dark blue and some yellow. What tradition permits them to substitute these colours for black? How come traditional observances are for women alone? This is blatant discrimination and subjection of women to upper caste patriarchal intolerance.

Either way, a review petition was filed in the Supreme Court. The court agreed to hear the petition giving hope to those who opposed the entry of women to the temple. During the hearing, the Travancore Devaswom Board, which administers the Sabarimala Temple, made a U-turn before the Supreme Court's Constitution Bench on the issue of women in the ten to fifty age group being allowed to enter the temple. The board, through senior counsel Rakesh Dwivedi, stated that it respected the judgement, and opposed the review petitions seeking reconsideration of the judgement delivered in 2018 lifting the bar on women in the specified age-group on entering the temple. 'People who are opposing entry of women in 10–50 age group should accept the Supreme Court verdict gracefully,' the Board urged the opponents.

The bench comprising Chief Justice of India Ranjan Gogoi and Justices A.M. Khanwilkar, Rohinton Fali Nariman, D.Y. Chandrachud and Indu Malhotra heard the arguments. The review petitioners were represented by senior advocates K. Parasaran, V. Giri, Abhishek Manu Singhvi, Shekhar Naphade and R. Venkatramani, each making brief oral submissions before the bench. The doctrine of essential religious practice, which enabled the majority of the judges to declare that the restriction on women's entry into the temple was not essential to Hinduism, was questioned by petitioners' counsel. Their argument being that the court cannot decide what was essential to a religion.

Even as the apex court reserved its judgement, the wind had gone out of the protestors' sails. And women had notched up a significant victory, reminding many of the dogged fight put up by Muslim women on the issue of instant triple talaq in the higher court. The court's judgement in the Shayara Bano versus the Union of India invalidated instant triple talaq giving much-needed relief from the whimsical actions of some headstrong men. Similarly, the court's September 2018 judgement told women that the court would take care of their interests in a society governed by patriarchal values. In fact, the activists, who had successfully contested the denial of space to women in the sanctum of the Haji Ali Dargah in Mumbai some five years before the Sabarimala verdict, had already expressed the hope that their success was a sign of things to change in Sabarimala. Their confidence did not prove misplaced. The Vavar Mosque holds out hope as well.

Hazrat Nizamuddin Auliya Dargah

'Hunuz, Dilli dur ast' (Delhi is still far away). So said Hazrat Nizamuddin Auliya as the Sultan of Delhi Ghiyasuddin Tughlaq returned from a military campaign in Bengal in 1325. The Sufi and the Sultan had been locked in a war of words. The Sultan though fond of Amir Khusrau, Auliya's trusted companion, threatened Auliya with dire consequences. The Sufi's words proved true. Delhi proved a bridge too far for the ruler. The Sultan could not reach Delhi with his carriage collapsing on a bridge near Delhi. Tughlaq's fate gave the status of a legend to the Sufi, and his words became part of the folklore. To this day, people throng the Dargah out of reverence: men, women, children, everyone. Women, did one say? Yes, they too are allowed inside the premises and can often be seen swaying in the spiritually enhanced atmosphere at the Dargah. Such is the reverence for Auliya that in the mid-1990s a fortnightly English magazine, with its editorial office in Nizamuddin, New Delhi, had to issue an apology to irate readers who objected to the absence of the word 'Hazrat' before Nizamuddin in the address published in the magazine. For them, the absence of the word 'Hazrat' before Nizamuddin meant a lack of respect for the much-revered saint.

Incidentally, for many devout people, the Nizamuddin Dargah is part of a trilogy of pilgrimage centres, beginning with Dargah Maa Saheba in Adchini in south Delhi, and going on to Nizamuddin before culminating in Ajmer, Rajasthan. The devout include people of all faiths, with Hindu men and women taking part in activities with equal fervour. They believe that before going on a pilgrimage to Moinuddin Chishti's Dargah at Ajmer, one has to pay respects at the Nizamuddin Dargah. And before going to Auliya's Dargah, one has to pay obeisance at Dargah Maa Saheba, which is the last resting place of Bibi Zuleikha, the mother of the 14th century Sufi. The Dargah used to be her residence in life. When she breathed her last in 1250, she was buried in her house only. Next to her grave in the complex is the grave of her daughter, Bibi Jannat. There is a mosque too. The men pray there. Five times a day one can see men file in neat rows for prayers, standing shoulder to shoulder. Women? They confine themselves to praying at the grave of Bibi and derive solace from it. At the Dargah though, there is nothing to hold back women from going up to the graves and offering rose petals besides chador to the mother of Auliya and his sister. The fact that they can touch and feel the last resting place means a lot to these women, they feel involved and a part of this place. Incidentally, according to some, they are afforded this right as the graves are of women, so the chance of *bepardagi* (being exposed) is not there. It is apt to recall that some clerics believe that women should not be allowed at a tomb or cemetery because the dead can see them without clothes!

Incidentally, there is an interesting anecdote involving Nizamuddin Auliya and his mother, which probably brings the devout to this Dargah. It is said that once Auliya was asked to attend the court of Sultan Qutb-ud-din who, after the death of the Khalji king Alauddin, had killed the heir apparent Khizr Khan, a disciple of Nizamuddin. His refusal to do so enraged the sultan who immediately declared if he did not come to attend the court on the first of the following month, he would have him brought forcibly.

> When the saint was informed, he went to the grave of his mother and stated that the king desired to harm him. If before the end of the month, his 'business was not settled', he would not come to visit her subsequently. The first of the month drew near and the shaikh's followers became increasingly concerned. The shaikh, however, derived assurance from his submission of the matter to his mother, herself a saintly person, and waited for whatever the future had in store. On the last night before the beginning of the new month, Khusrau Khan rebelled against the sultan and treacherously cut off his head. The issue was thus 'settled'. Nizamuddin Auliya was no longer required to visit the court.[6]

At Nizamuddin Dargah, things are different. While women are welcome, very welcome in most of the activities, some activities, such as establishing prayer or touching the grave of the saint, are male prerogatives. From different religions and regions, women come to the Dargah for their prayers. They soak in the ambience of the place and

---

[6] Aquil, Raziuddin. 2017. *Lovers of God: Sufism and the Politics of Islam in Medieval India*. New Delhi: Manohar Books.

attend qawwali sessions too. It is particularly energetic and colourful at the Basant Festival, which is held every year here and the place is awash with yellow as Sufi singers and even the *khadim*s dress up in yellow. The cross-religion festival is a major tourist attraction. Women, including many from the upper class who are otherwise seldom seen at a house of worship, are seen here. They mingle freely with women from other strata and communities, the Dargah acting as a great egalitarian avenue. Yet, when it comes to the time for prayer, a man announces, 'Ladies! Please clear the premises. It is time for prayers!' It is just assumed, and accepted, that only men can offer prayers in a congregation. And when they do so, women should not be within their eye level! As men begin to gather in a neat *saff* followed by another, women file out. Nobody protests.

Incidentally, that is not the only exclusion of women here. They are also not allowed to touch and stand at the last resting place of the Sufi. There is a marble lattice screen that shields the Sufi from women. Women can peep from behind these screens. Many touch the intricate jali work with sheer reverence and appear desperate to take the next step, touch and feel the grave. To see women rising to the tip of their toes and peeping behind the little openings in the screen is pretty common. While almost all women tend to take this exclusion in their stride as part of the tradition, some have started to speak up. Shailaja Tripathi, a Bangalore-based seasoned journalist, who always visits the Dargah on her trip to Delhi, says

> One has an elevating experience at the dargah. There is no discrimination on the basis of religion or gender. But not being able to touch the grave, having to look at the last resting place from behind a lattice screen makes one feel like a second class citizen. It makes one ask, 'Is my faith less than that of men?'

Despite this, she feels her prayers are answered, and it is essential to visit this Dargah before proceeding to Ajmer.

Incidentally, the khadims, those who help with the proceedings, are all men. 'Yes, only boys and even middle aged men are khadim at the dargah. It is the same at Ajmer too. There is no woman khadim or a khadima. But then when we cannot even touch the grave, how can they allow a khadima,' Tripathi reasons.

Other women, however, are not as ready to accept this gender bias. Till December 2018, nobody bothered. Women were happy to go to the Dargah, soak in the calm of the place without really caring about being denied the right to enter the innermost part of the spiritual retreat. That is until some students from Pune could not put up with this partial exclusion, and raised their voice in protest. They decided to seek legal redress too, claiming that the Dargah was a public place, and women had as much right to it as men. Upon their petition, the Delhi High Court issued notices to the Centre, Delhi's state government and the Hazrat Nizamuddin Dargah Trust seeking their viewpoint on women entering the Dargah's sanctum sanctorum. Women argued that there was no such exclusion at the Ajmer Dargah. And the Supreme Court had removed the discrimination prevalent in Sabarimala too.

In their plea, women contended that Nizamuddin Dargah is a public place and prohibiting women from entering the shrine is gender discrimination and, thus, highly unconstitutional. The plea cited the examples of two major Muslim shrines—Haji Ali Dargah in Mumbai and Khwaja Moinuddin Dargah in Ajmer—that allow entry of women.[7]

The Court is yet to pronounce its judgement. However, after Sabarimala has been opened to women of all ages, women here do hope that any remnants of gender prejudice will be removed from the Dargah. That hope is to be appreciated. But what about the caretakers? They are all men too. Remember those photographs of tall men at the hospice in yellow turbans or tall caps? That is another battle that is yet to be fought. If women can pray, why cannot they serve?

---

[7] Banka, R. 2018. 'Why Can't Women Enter Nizamuddin Dargah: Delhi High Court Notice to Centre, State'. Available at: https://www.hindustantimes.com/india-news/why-can-t-women-enter-nizamuddin-dargah-delhi-high-court-notice-to-centre-state/story-wbVuXieyME0U8bbYHy43HI.html (accessed on 25 April 2019).

Say, 'O My servants who have transgressed (by sinning), do not despair of the mercy of Allah. Indeed, Allah forgives all sins. Indeed, it is He who is the forgiving, the merciful.

—Surah Zumur [verse 53],
The Glorious Quran

CHAPTER 19

The Way Forward

Back in the early 1980s, a low-profile scholar of Islam, Mufti Abdul Dayam, saved a potentially hostile situation developing out of a case of instant triple talaq in the walled city of Delhi. A man had pronounced Talaq, Talaq, Talaq in a fit of rage, throwing his wife out of the house at midnight in the bylanes of Jama Masjid area. The wife slept at a neighbour's house. Next morning, she went to her parents' place, also in Delhi. A couple of days later, the man realised his folly and wanted her to come back to him. The wife too understood the consequences of the divorce for their little children—the couple had three children, all three under the age of ten. She also wanted to go back to him. For good measure, the man consulted a couple of clerics if he could take his wife back after pronouncing instant triple talaq at a single sitting, that too in a fit of rage. The clerics, at best, blessed with half knowledge, expressed their inability to do anything about it, pronouncing that the divorce had indeed taken place. The man was insistent he did not mean it. The woman was keen to forgive and forget. At that juncture, the case was brought to Mufti Abdul Dayam, known to have a more flexible approach to day-to-day issues in every day Islam. He sat the couple down, explained the responsibilities of marital life, admonished the man for his bout of anger, but, importantly, told them that their marriage was intact. They could go back and continue to live as husband and wife as multiple pronouncements of talaq in a single sitting meant only a single revocable divorce. Instead of the widely prevalent Hanafi ruling, he followed the Hanbali example under which divorce to be effective has to have a difference of at least one menstrual cycle between each pronouncement.

His enlightened ruling saved the day not just for the couple, but also for the community. It kept the media sharks away. A specific case of recklessness could not be pointed out as symptomatic of the community. In fact, in the much-talked-about Shayara Bano versus the Union of India and others verdict in August 2017, the problem could have been averted if the clerics that Bano and her parents consulted had been enlightened enough about the possibility of a woman seeking divorce through Khula rather than putting up with an intemperate husband demanding dowry. Bano's marriage would not have ended through instant triple talaq. The Supreme Court would not have had to come into the picture. And the nation could have concentrated on greater issues of poverty, security, equality, etc. But Bano never got the right guidance, and stayed ignorant of the right to end marital ties conferred upon women by the Quran. And what started as a little gust of wind became a storm that swept many off their feet.

Now, within the Muslim community in India, something similar is developing. It is not much more than a trickle at the moment. In times to come, it could well be a steady stream. A little later, it could sweep away all before it. Across the dingy lanes of Old Delhi, the wide roads of Noida, the chaotic bylanes of Mumbai and Ahmedabad, women are beginning to organise themselves. They are ready to dispel centuries of ignorance. They are keen to move away from the interpretations of the Quran made by the male clerics for centuries. They gather for lessons on the Quran. Most would have read the book in Arabic, but now they seek its meaning. Some try to learn Arabic, and many back it up with specific lessons on the commentary of the book. They are not satisfied with the age-old *tafsir* of Ibn Kathir, a 14th-century scholar whose work is still taught in the Islamic seminaries in India, Bangladesh and Pakistan. Women want to read Maulana Abul Ala Maududi, listen to Nouman Ali Khan, sit down and take notes when a recorded lecture of Farhat Hashmi plays in the room. They want to equip themselves with the reality of Islam. They exchange notes with their sisters while listening to Yasir Qadhi and Mufti Menk in South Africa or the US. They find a vast disparity between what these scholars tell them and the message of the Quran that they have been told since childhood. With the use of technology, they are breaking the male dominance in faith.

Strangely, around the same time, men, by and large, confine themselves to the centuries-old routine: going to the mosque, reciting verses in prayers that they usually do not understand and coming back home. In Taraweeh in Ramadan, they often stand to listen to a recitation of the Quran, which is often done at such a brisk pace that half of the words are incomprehensible. Many are, at the conclusion of a Taraweeh session on a day, in the dark about what they have just heard. They have no idea about the verses recited. All they know is that they have just heard some chapters of the Quran. At best, they know the name of the Surah. Women, meanwhile, pray at home. But it is changing. They are praying at home, yes, but in groups. After every *tafsir* class or after a Hashmi's lecture or listening to Khan on YouTube, they stand in a row for prayer; one of the women, usually the teacher, leads the prayer. Come Ramadan and these women gather at one of the neighbourhood houses or havelis to establish prayer in a group. Again, one of the women either recites the book from memory or reads aloud from the Quran she would be holding. At the conclusion of the Taraweeh, women are told about the verses they listened to. At times, they are told this after the conclusion of every four *rakat*s (cycles). As a result, they are able to concentrate better and also know what to expect in the next *rakat*. This way, women finish listening to the complete Quran in Ramadan in the special Taraweeh sessions. Men gather for the Taraweeh in large numbers at every mosque, whereas women do their much smaller *jamaat* close by. They give a message: If men have monopolised the mosques, we can develop our own prayer spaces. Also, unlike men who only listen to a quick recitation of the book in the mosque, women also discuss what they recite at the conclusion of their prayers. They attain knowledge. It empowers them. A handful of them are beginning to understand that the Quran asks every believer, whether male or female, to establish prayer. This is asked in the Quran around sixty times. No prayer can be established in isolation. In fact, there are two ways of establishing prayer. First is by safeguarding ones prayer from one time to another. In other words, if one has offered Fajr, one should desist from corruption or immoral deeds till the next prayer, i.e., Zuhr, and same from Zuhr to Asar and beyond. The second way of establishing prayer is in a group. Praying in isolation does not amount to establishing prayer. Any prayer concludes with a message of peace towards all, towards people on the right and people on the left. In every prayer, one says, 'We worship you alone; we seek help from you alone.'

The little informal classes of Hashmi and the small *saff* during the Taraweeh could challenge the male supremacy in the days to come, as women have started to take help from the Quran and Sunnah.

As in the case of instant triple talaq, it is for men to take corrective measures. And again, the community needs an alim (recognised scholar) with the open mindset of the mufti who saved the couple's marriage. In the absence of such an initiative, already, women such as V.P. Zuhra are seeking legal redress to the issue. In April 2019, a Muslim couple from Pune approached the Supreme Court, challenging the practice of prohibiting women from entering the mosques in India as being violative of Articles 14, 15, 21, 25 and 29 of the Indian Constitution.

Some twelve years earlier, around 2006, Rukiya had challenged the male monopoly of the mosques in Kerala. Then, a group of eleven women, led by Rukiya, petitioned the authorities seeking permission to enter all mosques in Ernakulam (Kochi). The Kerala State Wakf Tribunal ruled in their favour. However, despite the verdict, Muslim women in Kannur could not enter the mosque. While some mosques did open their portals to women, many equivocated. The verdict was in favour of women, but the residents around some of the mosques did not permit them despite the fact that the tribunal had studied the Quran, gone through some fatwas on the subject and consulted scholars before arriving at the decision. Soft-spoken Rukiya had confined herself to saying,

> Women have a right to pray in a masjid whenever they want. They should not be denied. All mosques in Saudi Arabia and West Asia permit women to offer prayers. Here, many local mosques are under the control of people who do not know much about Islam. Some maulanas who understand Arabic and the Quran permit women to go to a mosque, but in reality there are many who still stop women because of vested interests.

'They want to keep women in submission. It is important to base the fight for the right to enter the masjid within the fold of Islam. Anything permitted to women should not be denied. No innovation should be attempted,' she adds.

Indeed, her home state Kerala is emerging as the flag-bearer of Muslim women's rights with respect to mosques. Unlike most states of northern and central India, Kerala has a good number of mosques that are open to women. Yet much more needs to be done. After all, not all women stay in Kerala. It is for men to understand that Islam provides a prayer pyramid for all. It begins with the five daily prayers that one is supposed to say in the local mosque and interact with residents in the vicinity. On Friday, one is supposed to go to the bigger mosque, the Jama Masjid, and stay in touch with people beyond one's immediate neighbourhood. On Eid, one is supposed to go to the biggest place in the city, the Eidgah where one comes across people from all over the place. Then, once in a lifetime, one has to go for hajj where one sees Muslims from across the world. Step by step, stair by stair, the pyramid is made. Women are as much entitled to this pyramid as men.

Unfortunately, the reality is sadly and bitingly different. Hardly any Eidgah across north India keeps a provision for women, neither at the back, nor on the side. There is no reserved space for women. On Eid, they are, according to the widely prevalent view, just supposed to stay at home, cook, clean, bathe and deck up. Yet again, forgotten is the instruction of the Prophet on the subject. He is said to have asked women to take special care to attend the Eid congregation, buy a new shawl or cloak for the occasion. If they did not have a new one, he instructed them to wash the old one, but head for prayer. If the old one was beyond repair and cleaning, women were advised to borrow from a neighbour or friend, but still they had to head for prayer. Those who were undergoing the monthly periods were told to still go to the congregation and take part in the *dua* at the end. Today, women often dress up in their best clothes on Eid, but stay confined to their homes. Men go to the mosque or Eidgah, offer prayers, meet, hug and embrace their brothers and come back home. Women, meanwhile, just get busy with the chores. It has to change. A beginning has been made by Jamaat-e-Islami Hind which, realising that more women are gracing its precincts, has added a big prayer hall to its headquarters in Delhi, and plans to do the same with its mosques wherever the demand emerges. Then, we have private bodies taking initiative to provide avenues for women's congregational prayers. The Zakat Foundation of India organises Eid prayers for both men and women every year. Meanwhile, more mosques, such as Gulhar Wali Masjid in Delhi, Sona Bari in Kolkata and Jamaat Masjid in Parli, have started accommodating women. Even students in universities, such as Jamia Millia Islamia and Maulana Azad National Urdu University, have started to speak up for their sacred space. What's more, they have been granted the same too.

It is all in line with what the Prophet stood for. Prophet Muhammad was the seal of all the prophets. The Quran tells us through verse 31 of Surah Al'Imran, 'Say, [O Muhammad], "If you should love Allah, then follow me, [so] Allah will love you and forgive you your sins. And Allah is Forgiving and Merciful".' It quells all possibility of a debate on the subject. All those who point out that Imam Abu Hanifa was against women going to the mosques are either not speaking the complete truth or are not aware of the complete truth. Simple belief, as also logic states, that after Prophet Muhammad there will be no more prophets. Imam Abu Hanifa was not a prophet. Nor were Imam Shafi'i or Imam Malik and others. The Prophet not only permitted women to go to the mosques, he also asked men not to stop them. When women came with little babies in their arms, children who might cry in the middle of a prayer, he did not ask women to leave them behind. Instead, he made the prayer shorter, enabling women to attend to their babies soon. All he expected women to do was dress modestly, cover themselves fully and avoid using perfume, which might attract the attention of the opposite gender.

Any recourse to the contrary flies in the face of evidence from Islamic history. Women have been exempted, not prohibited from going to the mosques. The Prophet encouraged them to say the Friday and Eid prayers in a large congregation. A beginning can be made in the subcontinent by encouraging women to attend these special prayers, and men have to make space for them. No, not in a cursory room, like a dole handed out by political parties, but a place right behind them. Just as the Prophet did during his time. Until that is done, the patriarchal forces so well entrenched in the subcontinent will continue to prevail over the word of Allah and His Prophet. Society will remain paramount and faith subservient. Also, it is time for each mosque to declare that it is un-Islamic to prevent women from coming to the mosques. They should appoint women to the committees of the mosques. As of now, hardly any mosque committee has women members. It is men who decide the matters for both men and women. Also, in cases where mosques have logistic problems in making a separate entry and exit gate for women, women should be encouraged to have their own *jamaat*. Remember the case of Umm Waraqa who led prayers for women with the Prophet's permission? Ultimately, women's prayer space has to be restored, just as the Prophet had visualised it: behind men in the last row, in a position from where they can see the imam and not an obscure corner from where they can neither see the imam, nor hear the recitation clearly.

It is time for women to reclaim their sacred space.

CHAPTER 20

Women Now in Masjid

In the summer of 2023, little Yahya attended Taraweeh, the special prayers in Ramadan, for the first time in his life. Throughout the prayers, his mind was on everything but the prayer. He ran across the hall on the first floor of Ishaat-e-Islam Masjid in southeast Delhi's Abul Fazl Enclave, made friends with boys and girls his age. Prayer was a little picnic for him. Occasionally, he went and checked on his mother, Rida, just to be sure she was around. For Rida too it was her first Taraweeh in a masjid, standing shoulder to shoulder with women and listening to the recitation of the Quran.

In a unique, understated manner, the day marked a first for many women. They had grown up watching the men in their families head for Taraweeh an hour or so after breaking their fast. For years, they had heard with curiosity and envy the men discuss the chapters of the Quran recited in the masjid at the end of the day. But until recently they had not had an opportunity to experience it for themselves. When Rida and Yahya went to masjid, it broke many a tradition. Rida's mother, a practising doctor, had not attended either a Taraweeh or an Eid prayer inside a mosque till she was well into her fifties, and Rida too had had limited exposure to mosques. For Yahya it was a first, a boy accompanying his mother to masjid, as opposed to the usual team of father and son heading out for prayers.

The mosque, a relatively new addition, is a sign of changing times. The change is slow, perhaps very slow, but it is beginning to be felt. More and more mosques are opening their doors to women, some welcoming them with a space fully their own. Men's monopoly over mosques is coming to an end.

Shortly after this book was first published, two women students of Jamia Millia Islamia sent me a couple of photographs of the newly created space for them in the local Jama Masjid and a couple of other mosques in the neighbourhood. Having read the book, the women had met the management committee members and persuaded them to accommodate girls inside the mosque. The space allocated was unremarkable, dark, dingy and quite confined. But the women were jubilant. Though limited, the space for them was a major victory for their gender.

In the heart of Delhi, Moti Masjid in Connaught Place started welcoming women worshippers. A signboard outside the mosque (as seen in the summer of 2025) directs women to the first floor of the mosque. Like the men's zone on the ground floor, the first floor too has a proper arrangement for worship, copies of the Quran are available, as are facilities for lavatory.

Elsewhere, their sisters in faith had started a 'women-in-masjid' campaign of their own. In the autumn of 2022, women in sixteen cities, including Kolkata, Jamshedpur, Mumbai, Lucknow and Bhopal, gathered at a local mosque in their respective cities to offer Zuhr (afternoon) prayers on Sunday. Among the worshippers were women working in corporate offices, schoolteachers and housewives. Their socioeconomic and educational standards were varied, but they were united in their desire to reclaim their own space inside the mosques of India. A few days later, they turned up to offer the Friday prayers. 'Restricted to men over the years, a small group of 200 Muslim women would offer Friday prayers or Jumah Namaz at women-friendly masjids in Mumbai, Nagpur and 14 other cities across India on November 4,' *The Times of India* reported.[1]

---

[1] Ahmed, Sarfaraz. 2022. 'Muslim Women to Offer Friday Prayers in Masjids Across 15 Cities'. Available at: https://timesofindia.indiatimes.com/city/nagpur/muslim-women-to-offer-friday-prayers-in-masjids-across-15-cities/articleshow/95263154.cms (accessed 28 November 2025).

The initiative was planned under the Muslim Women in Masjid project started by the Muslim Women Study Circle, a collective formed during the anti-CAA protests in 2019.

Reading the writing on the wall, even the All India Muslim Personal Law Board (AIMPLB) submitted an affidavit in the Supreme Court in the Farha Anwar Hussan Shaikh case in February 2023 wherein it accepted women's right to pray in mosques. 'A Muslim woman is free to enter into a masjid for prayers. It is her option to exercise her right to avail such facilities as available for prayers in a masjid. ... It is submitted that the questions raised in the present petition are not in the background of state action. The practices of religion in the places of worship (which in the present matter are mosques) are purely private bodies regulated by "Muttawalis" of the mosques,' the affidavit, filed through advocate M.R. Shamshad, said.[2]

India Today quoted the AIMPLB as saying in the affidavit, 'The separation between chambers of men and women in many mosques is available to provide a comfortable and safe space for Muslim women who can pray in peace and unwind themselves during the most intimate spiritual activity, i.e nama[z].'[3]

Speaking to the author later, the board's spokesperson, S.Q.R. Ilyas, said, 'The women's demand for the right to offer namaz in masjid is justified. No verse of the Quran prohibits women from going to masjid. The only problem in some of the smaller mosques is the lack of space. I think over a period of time, arrangements will be made by such mosques also.'[4]

This is merely a beginning. Shortly after Rida and the Jamia women were soaking in the joy of praying in a masjid, Old Delhi's

---

[2] PTI. 2023. 'Entry of Women into Mosques for Namaz Permitted: Muslim Law Board'. Available at: https://www.ndtv.com/india-news/entry-of-women-into-mosques-for-namaz-permitted-muslim-law-board-3765581 (accessed 28 November 2025).

[3] Ojha, Srishti. 2023. '"Women Allowed to Offer Namaz in Mosque but..": Muslim Board Tells Supreme Court'. Available at: https://www.indiatoday.in/law/story/entry-of-women-into-mosques-for-offering-namaz-permitted-muslim-board-tells-supreme-court-2332644-2023-02-09 (accessed 28 November 2025).

[4] As told to the author in New Delhi, June 2025.

Jama Masjid, which had for long welcomed women worshippers, did an about-turn. The mosque barred single women from entering the mosque. *The Hindu* reported, 'In November 2022, the Jama Masjid in Delhi prohibited the entry of single women or women in groups inside the mosque premises. The authorities reasoned that some women fail to respect the sanctity of the place of worship, making videos there. "When women come alone, they indulge in improper acts, shoot videos. The ban is to stop this," reasoned the Masjid's spokesman.'[5]

As the media made a beeline to the mosque, the mosque management committee issued a clarification, stating, 'The ban excluded those women coming for worship, or those accompanied by their husband or families.'[6]

However, many continued to question the unilateral decision of the authorities, forcing Delhi Lieutenant Governor V.K. Saxena to step in to douse the fire. Following a meeting with the lieutenant governor, the mosque authorities withdrew the ban. Imam Ahmed Bukhari clarified, 'The masjid administration does not want to prevent anyone from worshipping inside.'[7]

A little later, women students at Nirmala College in Kochi, Kerala, were denied space to offer namaz in the college. The students requested for prayer space as the two mosques in the neighbourhood did not have space for them. 'A mosque is only 200 metres away from the college. Boys at the college go to the mosque at noon for prayers. However, the girls wanted to use a college room for their prayer, saying that they were not allowed at the mosque,' the principal told the media, even as he turned down the request for a separate prayer space on the college premises.

The principal's completely secular stand can be easily understood. He was under no compulsion to comply with the

---

[5] Salam, Ziya. 2022. 'On the Entry of Women in Masjid'. Available at: https://www.thehindu.com/news/national/explained-on-the-entry-of-women-in-masjids/article66202043.ece (accessed 28 November 2025).

[6] ibid.

[7] ibid.

women's request. The mosque management had no right to deny women worshippers. The exclusion of women, or indeed denial of their right to pray at the mosque, is against the teachings of the Quran as also the Constitution of India. It goes against the spirit of Article 14 of the Constitution which talks of the right to equality for all humans regardless of gender or religion. It goes against the word of the Quran which, through Surah Tawbah, verse 71, calls women partners of men.

These hiccups continue in the quest of Indian Muslim women to reclaim their space. But a beginning has been made, offering more than a ray of hope. Remember how despite opposition from many social and political quarters the New Delhi Jama Masjid designated a room for women worshippers in 2014, and Old Delhi's Jama Masjid too withdrew its ill-advised circular in 2022. And just as Covid-19 was subsiding, Jamaat-e-Islami Hind inaugurated a mosque in Delhi where some 2,500 women worshippers can pray at the same time. They come in droves for the Friday prayers, they come in hundreds for the Taraweeh namaz in Ramadan and in thousands for the Eid congregation, besides a handful for the daily prayers. The winds of change are blowing. Prepare to embrace the change. The written word matters.

Index

Note: The letter 'f' following locators refers to figures.

About the Author

Ziya Us Salam is a noted literary and social commentator. A student of history from Delhi University, he is engaged in building bridges of commonality between communities through recourse to the Quran and the Vedas.

Ziya has been associated with *The Hindu* for over twenty-five years and has been its Features Editor for North India editions for sixteen years. Currently, he is Associate Editor, *The Hindu*, and writes on sociocultural issues for the paper besides doing book reviews.

In 2019 Ziya published *Lynch Files*, a take on victims of hate violence, and *365 Tales from Islam*, a book that introduces Islam to children. His other books include *Of Saffron Flags and Skull Caps* (2018), a take on the challenges to the idea of India, *Till Talaq Do Us Part* (2018), a study of various divorce options available in Islam, and *Delhi 4 Shows* (2016), a study of cinemas since the talkie era began. He co-authored, with Anand Mishra, *The Lion of Naushera* (2025), an intimate biography of Brigadier Mohammed Usman.